Also by Dennis Adler

Porsche: The Road from Zuffenhausen

The Art of the Sports Car: The Greatest Designs of the 20th Century

The Art of the Automobile: The 100 Greatest Cars

Daimler & Benz: The Complete History

Ferrari

Ferrari

THE ROAD FROM MARANELLO

Dennis Adler

Foreword by **Luigi Chinetti, Jr.**

RANDOM HOUSE
NEW YORK

Published in the United States by Random House,
an imprint of The Random House Publishing Group,
a division of Random House, Inc., New York.

RANDOM HOUSE and colophon are
registered trademarks of Random House, Inc.

Archival black-and-white and new-model photography
provided courtesy of Ferrari North America and
Ferrari S.p.A., Italy, unless otherwise noted.

LIBRARY OF CONGRESS CATALOGING-IN-PUBLICATION DATA

Adler, Dennis
    Ferrari: the road from Maranello/Dennis Adler;
    foreword by Luigi Chinetti, Jr.
        p. cm.
    Includes index.
    ISBN 1-4000-6463-5
    1. Ferrari automobile—History. I. Title
    TL215.F47A35 2006   629.222'2—dc22   2005046697

Printed in China on acid-free paper
www.atrandom.com
9 8 7 6 5 4 3 2 1
FIRST EDITION

Book design by Keith Betterley

For Jeanne, whose love and encouragement have kept me writing books;

Luigi "Coco" Chinetti, for sharing great tales of the Cavallino Rampante;

and in memory of my late friend and writing partner T. C. Browne,

who began this Road from Maranello with me many years ago.

By Luigi Chinetti, Jr.

There have been many examples of iconic figures in the automobile and automobile racing world. One can think of the great Ettore Bugatti, whose blue racers and sports cars evoke images of carefree days in the 1920s, and whose personal mystique evoked class and aristocracy.

Bugatti's natural successor was Enzo Ferrari, who created his own mystique from relatively humble beginnings immediately after World War I, to the point where today, eighteen years after his passing, he is still revered as a man who pursued a dream of his own and created a legend in his lifetime.

For me it is a particular pleasure to be asked to write this Foreword to Dennis Adler's book because my father, Luigi Chinetti, shared almost every step of Mr. Ferrari's often turbulent career and helped to create here, in the United States, the legend that is Ferrari today.

Luigi Chinetti, Jr., photographed by the author outside one of the Maranello factories during a tour of Ferrari facilities in 1998.

Picture, if you will, the early 1920s: A war had ravaged Europe, leaving it in financial and political turmoil. The enthusiasm for automobile racing was still strong, and these times saw a young Enzo Ferrari competing with Alfa Romeo, alongside greats such as Giuseppe Campari and Antonio Ascari. Ferrari was quick and justified his place on the team with a win in the Coppa Acerbo in 1924.

My father began working with Alfa Romeo at exactly the same time, and fate was to bring him and Mr. Ferrari together and create a bond that existed for more than sixty years. How well my father knew Mr. Ferrari back in those days I do not know, but for sure the lives of both men were to become intertwined through their joint passion for automobile racing.

Around 1931, Alfa Romeo sent my father to Paris, where he was known as a specialist in the marque and was to open his own garage. It was there that he developed his

Chinetti, Jr., driving the 365 GTB/4 Daytona to victory at Le Mans in 1971.

skill in persuading wealthy young Frenchmen to buy Alfa Romeos and then helping them to race. One was Raymond Sommer, one of France's finest drivers. My father sold Sommer a 2300 Alfa Romeo, and with it the two of them won the 1932 Le Mans 24 Hour race.

It was to be the first of my father's three Le Mans wins. He won his second Le Mans in 1934, with another French driver, Philippe Etancelin, again in an Alfa Romeo, and he went on to compete in every Le Mans race until the beginning of World War II. It was a good life, but the political climate in Europe, with the rise of fascism in both Germany under Adolf Hitler and Italy under Benito Mussolini, was to bring an end to this special era.

The historians have amply stated that, during the 1930s, Enzo Ferrari had moved from actually racing cars to organizing and running many of Alfa Romeo's racing efforts under his own name, Scuderia Ferrari. He operated from his premises at 31 Viale Trento Trieste in the center of his hometown of Modena.

It was only when I was in my teens that I fully realized the importance of my having been present, as a little boy, at the famous meeting on a cold winter day in 1946 when my father and Enzo Ferrari sat down and created the seeds that were to develop into the Ferrari concern we know today. One must remember that Italy had been devastated by the war, and everything was in short supply; yet the two of them shared a dream that saw beyond those privations, to a time when people would indulge themselves once more in automobiles and racing. The agreement they came to that day was simple. Mr. Ferrari would build the cars, and Dad would commit to selling them. These were not just race cars but Ferraris for the street as well. The two men could see that selling the road cars would provide money for the racing exploits. It was a marriage made in heaven.

Despite the aforementioned problems, immediately after the war, Ferrari had the charm and charisma to motivate a workforce that was being heavily influenced by the Communist Party. Most companies in

Italy were beleaguered by lightning strikes, but his was spared much of this disruption.

As I understand it, my father returned to Paris as well during this period and, thanks to the network of influential friends he had built up before the war, was able to persuade two of the most successful French businessmen of the time, Michelle Paul Cavallier and Pierre Louis Dreyfus, to put much-needed capital into Ferrari, to help with production, and to create a company that it was hoped would become a success on both the circuits of the world and the public roads. Money was not wasted, and these investments enabled my father to participate in and win events such as the Spa 24 Hour race, the 12 Hours of Paris at Montlhéry, and, of course, the 1949 Le Mans 24 Hours.

During this period, Dad set out to make Ferrari known in the United States, and to this end he sold Briggs Cunningham the first Ferrari car imported to these shores. With that car Cunningham was to win at Watkins Glen in 1949, thus starting the Ferrari legend in America.

However, while introducing the Ferrari into the United States, Dad was also very instrumental in developing the marque in Europe, by presenting these early models, the 166 and the 212, in shows like Paris and Geneva. He arranged for Vignale to build, based on Giovanni Michelotti's designs, some of the most stunning, in my opinion, road cars of the era.

I think it was Ferrari's victories in long-distance sports car racing in late 1940s and 1950s that truly established the name. From then onward the Ferrari legend simply grew and grew. Ask enthusiasts today about the truly great cars of the postwar period, and the majority of those mentioned will carry the name Ferrari; the 250 GT Short Wheelbase, the Spyder California, the 250 GTO, all of them powered by the indestructible Ferrari V12 engine.

In 1956, Dad created the North American Racing Team (NART) in order to provide an umbrella under which our clients and promising new drivers could compete in various events both in the United

States and around the world. In this way we were able to bring these drivers, who perhaps did not have the financial backing to race at their potential level, together with other drivers who did. Both could profit from these partnerships, which gave one the chance to prove his mettle and the other the chance to improve himself through the garnered experience.

The team could be called a family of clients, drivers, mechanics, and volunteers, all out to strive for the best results possible. This relationship became fact when our car won Le Mans in 1965, giving Dad his first Le Mans victory as a team owner and Ferrari his last victory at Le Mans. I was lucky to catch the tail end of this period, before the circuits were somewhat emasculated by chicanes and Armco. To be able to race the fabulous Ferrari 312P cars at Sebring and Daytona was for me a privilege and a high point in my life. I state this even considering the fact that I was fortunate in winning, with Bob Grossman, my category at Le

Mans in 1971 and, in doing so, bringing the 365 GTB/4 Daytona into the history books.

Dennis Adler's book *Ferrari: The Road from Maranello* gives a wonderful portrayal of the fascinating story of Enzo Ferrari and his cars, and Dennis's photographs bring back many memories, not only for me but, I am sure, for every enthusiast of the Cavallino Rampante. It is also touching for me to see how successful my father's lifelong friendship and business relationship with Enzo Ferrari has been. It was not always a happy and contented partnership, but then you could not expect anything else from two such similar and remarkably self-confident men.

The name Enzo Ferrari will live forever in the history of the sporting automobile, and I feel privileged that our family played a part in a true-life automotive fairy tale.

Contents

Cisitalia—Realization of the Modern Sports Car

*There is a beginning to every story, and often the
beginning has little to do with how the story ends.
Such is the tale of the Cisitalia, a design in search of a car.*

Throughout the first five decades of the twentieth century, the automobile had captivated the French, the Germans, and the British, but it had somehow consumed the Italians. Driving and racing became such a national obsession that during the Great Depression, the Italian government purchased shares of Alfa Romeo stock to ensure the company's solvency through the 1930s! You see, it was a matter of national pride. Alfa Romeo was Italy's Motorsports champion. The four-time winner of France's *Vingt-quatre Heures du Mans* and the victor in ten consecutive Mille Miglias. Such unparalleled success could warrant no lesser fate than surviving the worst of economic times.

This national passion for motor racing drew a wealthy Italian industrialist named Piero Dusio into the sport after World War II. Like Enzo Ferrari, he had made his fortune selling war materials to the

In 1981 the Art Center College of Design cosponsored an exhibition with Fiat Motors of North America at the Pasadena Center in Southern California, celebrating Italian automotive design. The exhibition, *Carrozzeria Italiana,* was shown from May 23 to June 14. This was the first time many of these historic vehicles had been seen in the United States, and among the most exciting was an early Cisitalia 202 shown by Pininfarina.

The Cisitalia 202 was a landmark design and the centerpiece of the Carrozzeria Italiana. Said Pininfarina of his father's most important automotive design, "It was the best car he ever did. The Cisitalia was exhibited in the Museum of Modern Art in New York, and I think it set the pace for the design of sports cars."

Italian government. But unlike Ferrari, Dusio had found it profitable, even being on the losing side, and in 1946 he financed the development of an entire class of single-seat race cars, known by the graceful contraction of Consorzio Industriale Sportivo Italia, Cisitalia (eloquently pronounced "cheez-e-tahl-ya").

Dusio engaged the services of a talented Fiat engineer named Dante Giacosa, who designed a simple, Fiat-based race car that could be produced profitably in reasonable numbers. He also hired the former Fiat experimental engineer Dr. Giovanni Savonuzzi to put the car into production and none other than the great Piero Taruffi to test the first example. By August 1946, Cisitalia had produced seven of the new Tipo D46 Monopostos. In their debut race, the Cisitalias took the first three places, and in 1947 the legendary race driver Tazio Nuvolari steered his sports version of the Cisitalia to a second-place finish in

Left: The Cisitalia Granturismo Berlinettas produced in 1947 and 1948 were built atop a simple Fiat 1100S platform, with a four-cylinder inline monoblock engine and ordinary underpinnings, all soon forgiven when surrounded by hand-crafted Cisitalia bodies.

Below:
The author met with Sergio Pininfarina in 1981 for the first of their many interviews over the years. Pininfarina was fifty-five years old at the time and recalled with great humor his early days working for Mr. Ferrari.

the Mille Miglia. Orders for the D46 began to roll in. Now Dusio wanted to do the same for sports cars and underwrote the development of another Cisitalia model, the 202.

In the late 1940s, England, France, and Germany were still reeling from the destruction wrought by six years of war. Italy, however, being a country motivated by its love of wine, automobiles, and racing, was among the first to resume production. In 1946, Dusio paid the equivalent of one million francs to secure the freedom of Ferdinand Porsche from a French prison. The Porsche family repaid the favor by designing the scintillating four-wheel-drive Cisitalia twelve-cylinder Formula One Grand Prix car for Dusio and his friend Nuvolari. Dusio then spent the last of his fortune for the design and development of the 1947 and 1948 Cisitalia 202 sports cars.

For the Tipo 202, Savonuzzi had completed a preliminary layout at Dusio's request, but it was Battista Pinin Farina who finalized the architecture of the body and built the first two Cisitalia 202 coupes. When the first 202 appeared at the 1947 Villa d'Este Concours d'Elegance, the automotive world was astounded by both the simplicity of its design and its fresh approach to sports car styling. Not only did the Cisitalia send every automobile designer in the world back to the drawing board but it catapulted Pinin Farina into the postwar spotlight as the most renowned stylist on both sides of the Atlantic. In the 1950s he would become the first Italian to design cars for American automakers, including the magnificent 1952–54 Nash-Healey, the first American sporting car to have a chassis and suspension engineered in England (by Donald Healey) and a body designed and built in Italy.

The Cisitalia 202 was the finest expression of Pinin Farina's highly personal style, one that was both simple and functional, in contrast to the then current French design idiom, which was to overstate every line of a vehicle with coachwork, something Pinin Farina regarded as both complex and irrational.

The Cisitalia ignited within Italy the *granturismo* movements in which a body was conceived as a single profile rather than as a

A swept-back roofline and crowned rear fenders brought the enveloped body into harmony as it wrapped around the back of the car.

construct of separate panels, as in the traditional prewar blueprint of hood, fenders, body, and trunk being individual components. The sleek envelope styling exemplified by the Cisitalia gained momentum through the 1950s, particularly in the realm of high-performance sports car design, with smoothly flowing bodies that satisfied both the eye of the customer and the ideals of the engineer.

The Cisitalia Granturismo Berlinettas produced in 1947 and 1948 were built atop simple Fiat 1100S mechanicals, but one could overlook the languid four-cylinder in-line monoblock engine beneath the hood and the Italian automaker's ordinary underpinnings when they were

surrounded by the swept-back, handcrafted Cisitalia body. Although the little Fiat engine developed a mere 50 horsepower, the aerodynamic lines of the Cisitalia allowed the car to cheat the wind and reach a top speed of 100 miles per hour! Thus the Cisitalia became the symbol of the enveloping body, a school of design that would be emulated throughout Europe for the next two decades.

However, by 1949 Consorzio Industriale Sportivo Italia was broke. Dusio sold the remains and departed for Buenos Aires, along with the Grand Prix race car designed by Porsche. All that was left of his short-lived enterprise was a handful of stunning Cisitalia 202 Berlinettas.

The rake of the back-light as it fit into the sweeping rear of the body was another styling theme that would be perpetuated through the 1950s and '60s.

Bottom left:
The interior of the Cisitalia was also of Pininfarina's design and gave new brilliance to the otherwise pedestrian Fiat 1100S.

Bottom right:
Split windshields were still being used in 1947, but Pininfarina gave the Cisitalia a stylish curve at the top and bottom. The advent of one-piece, curved-glass windshields would be one of the very few improvements in 1950s sports car design not derived from the Cisitalia.

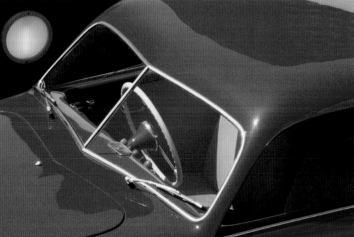

One can easily see the Cisitalia's influence on the first American sports car designed by Battista Pinin Farina, the 1953 Nash-Healey. Sergio Pininfarina noted that, "my father was also the first Italian to design an American-built car, the Nash Ambassador." (Nash-Healey from the Al Ruckey collection)

Below left:
Nash President George Mason insisted that the hybrid American-British-Italian sports car have a distinguishable 1951 Nash Ambassador grille. Pininfarina worked it into the design, although one might say the massive chromed grille with integrated headlights was a little heavy-handed compared with the sweet lines of the Cisitalia. In 1954, an even more attractive Nash-Healey Coupe was introduced.

Below right:
The sweeping fender-line of the Nash-Healey is almost identical to that of the 1947 Cisitalia 202.

Piero Dusio had bet the bank on a sports car and lost, but his money bought the most important design of the postwar era. The significance of the Cisitalia is exemplified by its selection for the 1951 New York Museum of Modern Art exhibition Eight Automobiles. It came to be regarded as the perfect example of sports car design. In 1972, Carrozzeria Pininfarina donated a 202 to MOMA's permanent collection, where the legendary Cisitalia now serves as an example of machine art.

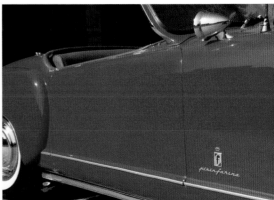

Ferrari

Luigi Chinetti had defied Ferrari's wishes. Enzo had said he would not build a spyder (convertible) version of the 275 GTB/4 Berlinetta (coupe). Chinetti thought otherwise. He ordered ten of the new Berlinetta models and sent them just down the road from Maranello to Sergio Scaglietti, the master coachbuilder who had produced so many stunning Ferrari bodies. There, the ten fixed-head cars were rebuilt and, with Scaglietti's mastery, reborn as 275 GTS/4 convertibles. The cars were all shipped to Chinetti's Greenwich, Connecticut, dealership and sold under the NART (North American Racing Team) name. In what could be deemed the final insult, Scaglietti had painted the very first car received by Chinetti a pale shade of sun yellow, or giallo solare, in Italian. When the non-factory-authorized Ferrari was scheduled to be raced at Sebring in 1967, Il Commendatore's ire could no longer be contained. Enzo did not believe yellow was a proper color for a competition car bearing his name—they had always been red, and he told Chinetti so in no uncertain terms. Shrugging it off, Chinetti replied in his Italian-laced English dialect, "Probobly, the scorers do not miss yellow so easily." Ferrari peered over his sunglasses, shook his head, and with a dismissive gesture replied indignantly, "Tu hai fatto un taxi" (You have made a taxicab!).

Chapter 1

Zero to Sixty Years—The Evolution of Ferrari

So many automobiles, so many names, but none can stir the imagination like the mention of Ferrari

In December 1946, one of the most important meetings in automotive history took place. It involved only two men, whose futures were to become intertwined and from whose combined efforts would emerge a marque that has come to be known the world over as the last word and, for many, the only word in sports cars—*Ferrari*.

After retiring as director of the legendary Scuderia Ferrari, Alfa Romeo's almost unbeatable factory-supported racing team, Enzo Ferrari established Auto Avio Costruzione to build racing cars under his own name. Unfortunately, no sooner had he started than Hitler's invasion of Poland in September 1939 ignited World War II.

Ferrari managed to earn a living during the war by building machine tools for the military, but with the end of the conflict and Italy defeated, there was little need for his tools, and even less demand for Italian race cars. Ferrari faced a grim future until he received a phone call on Christmas Eve 1946. It was an old friend, Luigi Chinetti. He was in Paris and wanted to visit Ferrari in Modena that night to discuss an idea.

Chinetti had worked with Ferrari at Alfa Romeo in the 1930s, and the two had become distant friends, Chinetti having moved to the United States before the war. He was visiting France and Italy that December when he got word of Ferrari's quandary. Chinetti knew of a market for Ferrari's race cars, back home in the United States, where wealthy sportsmen were raring to go motor racing now that the war was over. He explained this to Ferrari, and together they made a decision to enter into business; Ferrari would build the cars, and Chinetti would sell them. That was the beginning of a relationship that would become legendary.

Within a year Ferrari was producing a small number of twelve-cylinder race cars, and Chinetti was building the America distributorship.

The first Ferrari did not exactly receive rave reviews in the Italian press. After it appeared at Piacenza in 1947, one Italian newspaper referred to the Tipo 125 as "small, red, and ugly."

Road Cars and Race Cars

The difference between race cars and road cars in the early postwar era was strictly a matter of interpretation. The race cars could, for the most part, be driven on the road, and the handful of road cars produced were also suitable for racing. But, like the visually stunning 166 MM Barchetta, most were far from practical. What Ferrari needed most for his nonracing clientele was a convertible, and in 1949 the first Ferrari convertible made its debut at the Geneva Motor Show.

The next significant turning point in Ferrari road car production came in 1951, with the introduction of the Tipo 212. Whereas racing had once been Enzo Ferrari's sole raison d'être, the design and production of road cars had now taken on equal importance.

Among the most stylish of the early Ferrari road cars were those built by Carrozzeria Vignale. The luxurious Vignale 212 Inter was intended as a touring car but also managed to acquit itself quite well when pressed into competition. A pair of 212 Inters finished first and second in the 1951 Carrera PanAmericana, with Piero Taruffi and Luigi Chinetti in the lead car, and Alberto Ascari and Luigi Villoresi close behind.

Between 1948 and 1952, Ferrari continued to increase the swept volume of his twelve-cylinder engines, with each succeeding version more fortunate in competition than the last and possessing increasingly attractive coachwork by Touring, Pinin Farina, and Vignale.

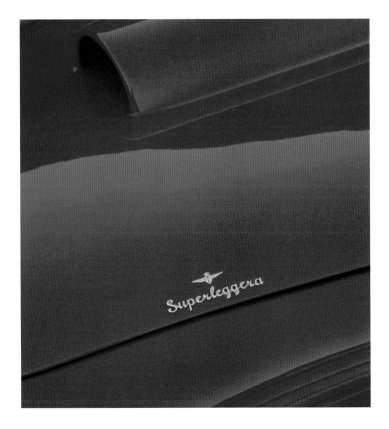

The Barchetta featured a dramatic hood scoop to draw air into the engine compartment. The Superleggera script on the side of the hood indicated the Touring's lightweight coachwork had been used in the car's construction.

The 225 S or Sport followed the design of the 212 Inter, with a Colombo short-block V12, now with a swept volume of 2.7 liters. The 225 S shared the 212's chassis, with a double wishbone, transleaf spring front, and rigid axle, semielliptic spring rear suspension, and the same physical dimensions.

Headlong into the 1950s and 1960s

By the mid-1950s, Ferrari was producing a substantial number of road cars, and the separation between them and those built for com-petition was becoming more clearly defined. However, to say that there was a "production" Ferrari in the 1950s would still be a bit of a stretch. The design and construction of bodies remained the work of the individual carrozziera.

During the early part of the 1950s, Ferrari road cars varied from the 212 series (which remained in production until October 1953) through the 340 America (1951–52), 342 America (1952–53), and 375 America, introduced in 1953. These were the first road cars to carry the Ferrari name successfully beyond Italy, particularly to the United

At Spa-Francorchamps in 1949, Luigi Chinetti drove a 166 MM to victory in the twenty-four-hour event.

The 212 Inter and Export models bodied by Vignale were the height of Italian styling in the early 1950s. The styling influence of the Cisitalia could still be seen.

Although Pinin Farina had created several significant cars for Ferrari by 1956, the design of the 410 Superamerica was perhaps the most important in cementing the bond between these two great companies. Only nine examples of the 410 Superamerica were produced by Pinin Farina in the original 1956 style, but the influence of the car's groundbreaking design would be felt for years to come.

Beneath the Superamerica's long hood was another marvel, a Lampredi-designed V12 increased to almost 5 liters in displacement (302.7 cubic inches) and delivering a wheel-spinning 340 horsepower at 6,000 revolutions per minute. Versions produced in 1958 and 1959 developed a chest-swelling 400 horsepower at 6,500 rpm. The Lampredi V12 said *ciao* to the Cadillac- and Chrysler-powered race cars as it dusted them off in sports car competition.

States, where Luigi Chinetti had now established Ferrari as the most prestigious line of imported sports and racing cars in the country.

Upon entering the American market, Ferrari discovered that, though American cars were heavy, chrome-laden machines, their engines were very powerful, with large displacements and tremendous horsepower. When big Cadillac and Chrysler engines were used to power race cars like the British Allards, those cars were outrunning Ferrari in sports car competitions. To level the playing field, Enzo embarked upon the design of a comparable V12 with tremendous horsepower and displacement. It would come to be known as the 410 Superamerica.

Ferrari's 225 S is one of the most beautiful race cars ever designed by Carrozzeria Vignale. A listing of serial numbers shows that about twenty were built during the model's single year of production, 1952, and that all but one had coachwork by Vignale.

Below:
With a need to build road cars as well as race cars, Ferrari introduced its first convertible in 1949. Bodied by Stabilimenti Farina, it was shown at the Geneva Salon in 1949. Luigi Chinetti, Sr., was there to debut the first Ferrari ever displayed at a motor show outside Italy.

The Great Road Cars

The lineage of the 250 GT series is replete with one legendary car after another, more so than any other model in Ferrari history. Topping that list are cars with unforgettable names like Tour de France and GTO. The Tour de France, a name affectionately given to the early 250 GT models following their domination of the ten-day race in 1956, remained in production until 1959, by which time a new benchmark Ferrari model, the 250 GT Short Wheelbase Berlinetta, was waiting in the wings.

Ferrari unveiled the 250 GT SWB at the Paris Motor Show in October 1959. Built on a 94.5-inch wheelbase, its overall length was only 163.5 inches (13.6 feet). The blunt-looking fastback carried a classic Colombo-designed 60-degree, 3-liter V12 beneath its elongated hood. As a result of the

The 410 Superamerica redefined the Ferrari image in the early 1950s with a high-performance V12 designed to compete with America's big V8s. This is a Series III example, the last of twelve built between 1958 and 1959. With the highest output of the 410 Superamerica line, a rousing 400 horsepower from its Lampredi-designed 4.9-liter engine, this was the most powerful road car Ferrari had yet delivered into the hands of its customers. (Dave Cummins collection. Photos by Don Spiro)

car's design, shorter overall length, reduced weight, and increased output—280 horsepower at 7,000 revolutions per minute versus 260 horsepower at 7,000 rpm for the Tour de France—the Short Wheelbase Berlinetta was faster and handled better than its famous predecessors. All of the cars were equipped with four-speed synchromesh gearboxes, and later models were offered with electric overdrive. The 250 GT SWB was also the first GT Ferrari sold with disc brakes.

The now coveted 250 GT SWB Spyder California made its debut at the Geneva Salon in March 1960. These examples were equipped with new heads and larger valves, increasing output by 20

The styling influence of the 410 Superamerica can be seen in this 1958 250 GT Tour de France race car.

Below:
The Pinin Farina styling established by the 410 Superamerica can still be seen in the 250 GT Spyder California.

horsepower to 280 at 7,000 rpm. The track was widened on SWB models, which were also the first to switch from lever-type shock absorbers to adjustable telescopic units. The cars were also offered with a longer wheelbase, the LWB.

The Spyder California, in either wheelbase, was one of the first Ferrari "driver's cars," capable of exceptional speed and handling yet comfortable and luxurious enough for daily use. The last example, 4167 GT, was sold in the United States in February 1963.

With the debut of the 250 GT Berlinetta Lusso, Pininfarina had at once established a new level of style and luxury for Ferrari. Here was an awe-inspiring stretch of automobile that even rivals Maranello's latest. Production of this now highly collectible GT totaled only 350 from its introduction at the Paris Motor Show in October 1962 until

The 250 GT Short Wheelbase Berlinetta was the consummate race and road car in the late 1950s and early 1960s. Unveiled at the Paris Motor Show in October 1959, the 250 GT SWB was built on a 94.5-inch wheelbase with an overall length of only 163.5 inches, (13.6 feet). The blunt-looking fastback carried a classic Colombo-designed sixty-degree, 3-liter V12 beneath its elongated hood. Interior appointments were luxurious by Ferrari standards of the era.

the last body left the Scaglietti atelier in 1964. When the last Lusso pulled away from Maranello, it marked the conclusion of the 250 GT era. Over a period of ten years, the 250 GT designation had been applied to nearly 2,500 cars.

The Quintessential Ferrari—275 GTB

The most charismatic road car to come from Maranello after the 250 GT Berlinetta Lusso was the all-new 275 GTB. Introduced as a two-cam model in 1964, it was the first of Ferrari's now legendary '60s-era Berlinettas offered to customers in touring or racing configurations. Equipped with the Colombo-designed sixty-degree V12 displacing 3,286 cubic centimeters and dispensing 280 horsepower at 7,600 revolutions per minute, the 275 GTB was the ultimate expression of Ferrari's ideology: a road car suitable for racing that gave up little, if anything, to competition models.

The 275 GTB had been powered by a twin-cam engine but that

was not for long. In 1966 a four-cam model, the 275 GTB/4, was introduced. Sergio Pininfarina's exotic styling for both the 275 GTB and 275 GTB/4 captured with great success the better elements of the competition-built 250 GTO as well as, at the rear, the styling of the GTB Lusso. The 275 GTB/4 may be as close to perfection as any sports car has come. The veteran race driver Phil Hill described the 275 GTB/4 as "like a boulevard version of the GTO."

The 275 GTB/4 was followed by the groundbreaking 365 GTB/4, which deposed the traditional Ferrari grille for a new aerodynamic, wraparound look with headlights concealed behind a clear strip of Perspex plastic. This is the original prototype built by Pininfarina.

Far left:
Among the rarest of the landmark Ferrari 275 GTB models was the *competizione* model designated 275 GTB/C. The car featured a lighterweight all-alloy body construction.

Out with Tradition—The Daytona

Ferrari had established a "style" with the Touring Barchetta that gave every car from Maranello a menacing look, with wide, dark grilles that seemed to consume the fronts of the cars and looked as if they could just as easily consume the cars in front of them. However, for the new 365 GTB/4 Daytona, Sergio Pininfarina and his staff were about to take a detour.

Aerodynamics was the new order in the late 1960s, and this dictated a new front end design for Ferrari. The Daytona did away with the traditional oval grille, replacing it with a sleek, aerodynamic visage that also eliminated conventional headlights. For more than twenty years the headlights had been a part of the fender design, but with the 365 GTB/4 there were no front fenders, at least not in a traditional sense. For this model, Pininfarina chose to set the headlamps back under a single band of clear plastic, which blended

Sitting still or racing down the highway, the 365 GTB/4 Daytona rewrote the book on Ferrari styling.

with the line of the front end. The design was dazzling and adventurous, breaking with all previous canons of Ferrari styling.

The Mid-Engine Ferrari

Racing has been the foundation for nearly all of Maranello's advancements in the design of road cars. One of the most significant was the development of the boxer engine in 1964. Ferrari's first flat-opposed (180-degree) boxer engine was a twelve-cylinder, 1.5-liter Formula One engine with 11:1 compression ratio, Lucas fuel injection, and an output of 210 horsepower at 11,000 revolutions per minute.

Ferrari's first mid-engine production sports car (discounting the Dino) was the 365 GT4 Berlinetta Boxer. Introduced in 1974, it was equipped with a 4.4-liter production version of the competition engine mounted behind the driver and ahead of the rear axle. Output was a rousing 380 horsepower at 7,200 rpm. This would be only the first of an entire generation of rear-engine, twelve-cylinder models that would remain in production for more than twenty years.

The 365 GT4 Berlinetta Boxer was the first Ferrari road car since

The mid-engine Ferraris were the closest Maranello came in the 1970s to putting drivers behind the wheel of a road-going race car. The 512 Berlinetta Boxer remains one of the most spectacular of all Ferrari models.

Ranking the 250 GTO among the greatest Ferrari race cars ever built is something everyone, even non-Ferrari enthusiasts, will agree upon. This example is perhaps the greatest of them all, the car that won at Le Mans in 1963.

Opposite:
The 308 GTB, GTS and later 328 series GTB Berlinetta and GTS Spyder (shown) were among the most popular and affordable of the road cars produced by Maranello in the 1970s and 1980s.

the 275 GTB/4 actually to give drivers a taste of what a race car felt like. It remained in production until late in 1976, when the new 512 Berlinetta Boxer was introduced. The body styling of the 512 was almost identical to that of its predecessor. Pininfarina's revised styling added a chin spoiler, or air dam, beneath the egg-crate front grille, and air ducts on the lower body sides forward of the rear wheels. The new model employed the same blended media construction as the 365 GT4 BB. The use of glass fiber led to the most distinctive and memorable styling characteristic of both the 365 and the 512, a solid

division line between the upper and lower body panels. On the 365, the lower part was always painted matte black. The two-tone color scheme became an option on the 512 BB.

Both the 365 and 512 boxers were raced by private entrants, but their time in the sun was brief and the racing effort short-lived. They were by far the best road cars Ferrari had brought to market up to that time. Thirty years after the introduction of the 512 BB, with its razor-edge styling and incomparable mid-engine layout, it remains one of the most distinctive of all Ferrari.

In 1987 Ferrari celebrated its fortieth anniversary with a new model, the F40, a lightweight Berlinetta powered by a twin-turbocharged V8. The most sensational road car built up to that time, it had a transparent engine cover that revealed a view of raw Ferrari horsepower as never before. By the time the cars were sold out, they had increased in price from the $250,000 originally asked by the factory to nearly $1 million.

Evolution in design has led to many of the most outstanding and best-loved road cars, but none became more ubiquitous than the 308 GTB and GTS, the most recognized Ferrari ever produced, thanks in part to Tom Selleck and his *Magnum P.I.* television series. Moreover, Ferrari enthusiasts found this the most practical driver Maranello had thus far built.

Pininfarina stylists combined the best attributes of the 246 Dino and 365 GT Berlinetta Boxer in the 308's design. Suspension was all independent in the then traditional

Ferrari layout, and the cars were powered by a four-cam, ninety-degree V8 engine mounted transversely just ahead of the rear axle. The 308 offered a spirited 255 horsepower at 7,700 revolutions per minute and drove through a five-speed transmission. An open version of the 308, with a removable roof section similar to that used on the 246 Dino and Porsche 911 Targa, was added to the line in 1977.

The longest running model in Ferrari history, the 308 continued on into the 1980s in improved versions, the 308GTBi, 308GTB Qv (quattrovalve), and 328 Berlinetta and Spyder.

Today's Ferrari

The latest generations of Ferrari, beginning with the fortieth-anniversary F40 in 1987, have become the signature cars of Sergio Pininfarina. "I have had the pleasure of meeting many people at the Concours, [Pininfarina is a judge each year at the prestigious Pebble Beach Concours d'Elegance], and they tell me that they own a new Ferrari, or an old one, and then they say, 'Thank you for what you have done.' There is no satisfaction in the world better to me than this."

With the company not wanting a reprise of the F40 debacle caused by speculators buying cars for resale as the supply ran out, F50s were delivered to selected customers on lease; only after the term of the lease could they be resold. At nearly $500,000 a copy when new, and with every one of the 349 cars built through 1997 pre-sold, Ferrari achieved both price control and exclusivity.

Among the most exciting of contemporary models is the 550 Maranello. When introduced in 1997, it was the first front-engine Berlinetta to be built since the 375 GTB/4 Daytona. Designed by Pininfarina, this graceful new sports car readied Ferrari for the turn of the century.

His feelings about Ferrari, he says, are difficult to describe in Italian, impossible in English. "When I see all these red cars in the sunshine, I see one lifetime of work. In one way I feel very proud and, in another, very conscious of the importance of my position [and Pininfarina's] with Ferrari for the future." That future has taken the form of cars like the 456 GT 2+2, F 355 Berlinetta and Spider, the fiftieth-anniversary F50, the 550 Maranello, the Modena, Enzo, and the new 575 Maranello, among others.

As Ferrari nears its sixtieth anniversary in 2007, the world awaits another legendary anniversary car and a new generation of Ferrari road and race cars for the twenty-first century.

One of the latest models, the 575 Maranello, takes the original 550 one step further, with even more power and refined styling.

Among twenty-first-century Ferrari models is the new, limited-production Ferrari Scaglietti.

Chapter 2

Enzo Ferrari's Venture—An Independent Decision

"My return to Modena…represented…an attempt to prove to myself and to others that, during the twenty years I was with Alfa Romeo, not all my reputation was second-hand and gained by the efforts of others. The time had come for me to see how far I could get by my own efforts."

—*Enzo Ferrari*

It is unlikely one could travel the world today and find any country, any town or city, where the name Ferrari is not known. Even in the 1930s, long before he had a company bearing his own name, Enzo Ferrari was well-known as the mastermind behind Alfa Romeo's factory-supported racing team—Scuderia Ferrari.

Born in Modena, Italy, on February 18, 1898, Enzo was the son of a local metal fabricator. When Enzo was ten, his father took him and his brother, Alfredo Jr., to an automobile race in Bologna. Enzo watched intently as Vincenzo Lancia and Felice Nazarro fought for victory in the 1908 Circuit di Bologna. "This race made a great impression on me," wrote Ferrari. After sitting through several more, young Enzo was certain that he wanted to become a race driver, but at age eighteen his world fell apart when he lost both his father and his older brother. "My father," wrote Ferrari, "died

Now a respected driver for Alfa Romeo, a more serious looking Enzo Ferrari was photographed with his mechanic, Eugenio Siena, at the May 1924 Pescara-Coppa Acerbo.

In 1920, an exuberant Enzo sits behind the wheel of an Alfa Romeo race car.

Top right:
Ferrari and mechanic Siena pictured in the 1924 Alfa Romeo RL Targa Florio at the Pescara-Coppa Acerbo, Circuito dell'Aterno, July 13, 1924.

at the beginning of 1916 of one of those bouts of pneumonia that the doctors today can defeat in a few hours. My brother, Alfredo, too, died the same year of a malady caught whilst doing military service work. I found myself quite alone and at a turning point in my life." Enzo entered the army and spent World War I working as a farrier. He contracted the flu during the great epidemic of 1918 and barely survived. After that, he decided to fulfill his one childhood dream, that of becoming a race car driver.

Discharged after the war, he entered his first major competition in 1919; it was the grueling Targa Florio, which was run through the treacherous Sicilian mountains. Driving for Costruzioni Meccaniche Nazionali, C.M.N. for short, he finished a respectable ninth

place, what one might describe as a trial by fire for the twenty-one-year-old Ferrari. It was a most unusual race, as he recounted. Co-driving with his friend Ugo Sivocci, Ferrari found himself in a blizzard atop the Abruzzi mountains. "[We were] facing a risk we had never bargained for: we were chased by wolves! These were put to flight, however, by shots from the revolver which I always kept under the seat cushion and by the arrival of a group of road gangers armed with torches and guns." Ferrari and Sivocci would have finished higher but were detained by a roadblock set up outside Campofelice by the carabinieri (Italian police) to stop traffic while the president of Italy, Vittorio Emanuele Orlando, made a speech. Afterward they were permitted to go but were caught behind the presidential motorcade until it turned onto another road. Ferrari recalled, "When we eventually arrived, the timekeepers and spectators had all disappeared with the last train to Palermo; a *carabiniere*, armed with an alarm clock, was patiently recording the times of the last arrivals, rounding them off to the nearest minute. On Monday, I went round to see Don Vincenzino Florio [the event's organizer]. 'Well, what are you grumbling about?' he said in his usual blunt way. 'You were late, you risked nothing, and we are even making you a present of including you in the classification!' I was given ninth place, which was supposed to represent a success, albeit a small one. That was Don Vincenzino Florio! I considered him as a preceptor and, later, counted him as a friend."

Through Sivocci, Enzo found employment with Alfa Romeo later that year, beginning a career with the renowned Italian automaker that would last twenty years.

His youth, determination, and fearless bravado behind the wheel made Ferrari a strong competitor. In 1920 he returned to Sicily and finished second in the Targa Florio, driving one of the 4.5-liter, four-cylinder cars, after which he came under the patronage of Giorgio Rimini, Nicola Romeo's aide and director of sales and racing. In 1923, Enzo was racing and winning at the famed Circuit of Sivocci at Ravenna when he met the father of the legendary Italian World War I flying ace Francisco Baracca. The senior Baracca was so enamored with the courage and audacity of young

Ferrari and riding mechanic in the cockpit of an Alfa Romeo RL Targa Florio model in 1924.

Ferrari that he presented Enzo with his son's squadron badge, the famous Cavallino Rampante, the prancing horse on a yellow shield. This was to become Ferrari's symbol, first as the head of Alfa's racing team, Scuderia Ferrari, and later that of his own company.

Ferrari was declared a full factory driver for Alfa and was scheduled to compete in the most prestigious race in Europe, the French Grand Prix. What happened next has never been explained, but Ferrari suffered what those close to him called a "crisis of confidence" and withdrew from the biggest race of his career. Rather than leave the team, however, he became Giorgio Rimini's right-hand man. He didn't race again until 1927 and continued to race occasionally until 1931, as well as manage the Alfa team. He said, "I resolved to withdraw from active participation in motor racing in January, 1932,

Ferrari is surrounded by Alfa Romeo drivers and mechanics after winning the 1924 Pescara-Coppa Acerbo, Circuito dell'Aterno.

when my son Dino was born. My last race of the previous season had been on the 14th of June, when I competed in the Bobbio–Monte Penice, up the hills to the south of Piacenzia. I had a new 2300cc Alfa Romeo eight-cylinder designed by [Vittorio] Jano, and won first place. That day, however, I made a promise to myself that, were I to have a son, I would give up driving and go in for something in the way of organization and business. I kept that promise."

The turning point in his life that helped make this decision possible had come after Alfa temporarily withdrew from racing in 1925 and turned to Ferrari to assist their racing clientele with mechanical support, delivery of cars, and whatever other services were required. In exchange Ferrari was guaranteed technical assistance from the factory, which purchased stock in his new company, Scuderia Ferrari.

The world had met Enzo Ferrari at the 1919 Targa Florio but it came to *know* him as a result of the other great Italian race, the Mille Miglia. Said Ferrari, "When I talk about this race, I feel quite moved, for it played such a big part in my life. I knew it as a driver, a

team director, and a constructor. In fact, this race not only provided enormous technical advances during its three decades, it really did breed champions. The race was an epoch-making event, which told a wonderful story. It created our cars and the Italian automobile industry and permitted the birth of grand touring cars, which are now sold all over the world, fully justifying the old adage that motor racing improves the breed."* During his tenure with Alfa Romeo, Ferrari's team won the Mille Miglia ten times!

Enzo Ferrari had created the largest racing team ever assembled by one individual, with Giuseppe Campari and Tazio Nuvolari as his star drivers. In all there were fifty drivers being supported by the Scuderia, which in its first full season competed in twenty-two

events, winning eight outright and scoring high in several others. It was a very good beginning.

Alfa Romeo continued to support Scuderia Ferrari as the official racing department of the factory throughout the 1930s. And when financial troubles arose because of the Depression, the Italian racing tire manufacturer Pirelli interceded and convinced Alfa to continue supporting the Scuderia. The Italian government even stepped in, as previously mentioned, and purchased shares of Alfa Romeo stock to keep the company solvent.

Shortly after the birth of Enzo's first son, Alfredo (named after Ferrari's late father and brother, but later known by the nickname Dino), the millionaire sportsman and race driver Count Carlo Felice

* Andy Marks, "The Great Races," published in *Car Collector Magazine*, 2005

On May 11, 1947, the very first car bearing the Ferrari name appeared in public in Italy. Sports cars were practicing for racing at Piacenza, and two versions of the new Ferrari Tipo 125 S 1.5-liter sports car were shown. One was a simple, two-seat Spyder Corsa, later referred to in an Italian newspaper as "small, red and ugly." The example shown, from the David Sydorick collection, is a 166 Spyder Corsa, one of the very first Ferrari race cars built in 1947.

Trossi decided to invest in Scuderia Ferrari. He later became president of the Scuderia, thus freeing Ferrari to devote his total attention to the team, which was coming up against extraordinary competition from Mercedes-Benz and the German Auto Union.

The late 1930s were not as rewarding for the Scuderia as Ferrari and Trossi had anticipated. The Germans were almost unbeatable. With the exception of Nuvolari's victory in the 1935 German Grand Prix, major victories for Scuderia Ferrari and Alfa Romeo were few and far between through the rest of the decade, as Mercedes and the Auto Union continued to dominate.

In his memoirs, Enzo wrote of Nuvolari's incredible driving skills. With Ferrari as a passenger in Nuvolari's race car, the great Italian *pilota* was prerunning the Three Provinces Circuit, upon which he had never competed. Writes Ferrari: "At the first bend, I had the clear sensation that Tazio had taken it badly and that we would end up in a ditch; I felt myself stiffen as I waited for the crunch. Instead, we found ourselves on the next straight in perfect position. I looked at him: his rugged face was calm, just as it always was, and certainly not the face of someone who had just escaped a hair-raising spin." Ferrari continued to note that he experienced the same sensation through

the next several bends. "By the fourth or fifth bend I began to understand; in the meantime I noticed that through the entire bend Tazio did not lift his foot from the accelerator, and that, in fact, it was flat on the floor. As bend followed bend I discovered his secret. Nuvolari entered the bend somewhat earlier than my driver's instincts would have told me to. But he went into the bend in an unusual way: with one movement he aimed the nose of the car at the inside edge, just where the curve itself started. His foot was flat down, and had obviously changed down to the right gear before going through this fearsome rigmarole. In this way he put the car into a four-wheel drift, making the most of the thrust of the centrifugal force and keeping it on the road with the traction of the driving wheels. Throughout the bend the car shaved the inside edge, and when the bend turned into the straight the car was in the normal position for accelerating down it, with no need for any corrections."

Ferrari went out with Nuvolari repeatedly in the 1930s, remarking that "each time I seemed to be climbing into a roller coaster and finding myself coming through the downhill run with that sort of dazed feeling that we all know."

In 1937, Ferrari found himself with a new dazed feeling. Alfa Romeo decided to bring the racing department back in-house, appointing Ferrari Direttore Sportivo under the management of the new Alfa engineering director, Wilfredo Ricard. There was an almost immediate acrimony between the two men. Ricard was a

The 166 MM Touring Barchetta was the first sports car ever shown on a Ferrari chassis. The aggressive body was set atop the patented Superleggera welded tubular steel frame on a wheelbase of 2,200 millimeters (86.6 inches). Track measured 1,270 millimeters (49.8 inches) front and 1,250 millimeters (49.2 inches) rear. The front suspension used Ferrari independent A-arm design, supported by a single transverse leaf spring. The rear utilized a live axle with semielliptic springs and parallel trailing arms on each side. Shock absorbers were the Houdaille hydraulic lever action type. The car pictured was originally raced by Luigi Villoresi and later sold to the race driver and Ferrari importer Luigi Chinetti.

Spaniard with impressive credentials. He was a gifted speaker, fluent in five languages, and he quickly captured the political support of Alfa management. Said Enzo, "He impressed Ugo Gobbato [Alfa Romeo's manager], I believe, with the way in which he presented his plans, with the clear and elegant manner in which he expressed himself, with the ease in which he pursued publications of every country, and finally, with the air of authority with which he knew how to submit explanatory diagrams prepared by a young graduate he had engaged as secretary for the Special Studies Office, namely Ing. [engineer] Orazio Satta, later to become Alfa Romeo's design manager and the virtual father of the *Giulietta* car." Though his appraisal of Ricard's credentials sounded enviable, Enzo found his new boss a strange individual with whom he could not work.

"With sleek, oiled hair and smart clothes that he wore with a somewhat Levantine elegance, Ricard affected jackets with sleeves that came down far below his wrists and shoes with enormously thick rubber soles. When he shook hands, it was like grasping the cold, lifeless hand of a corpse," remarked Ferrari. When he finally decided to inquire about the unusual shoes Ricard's reply left Ferrari almost speechless; the director answered straight-faced and deadly serious, "A great engineer's brain should not be jolted by the inequalities of the ground and consequently needed to be carefully sprung."

Ricard proved to be a buffoon after several of his designs failed, but Ferrari, having been Il Commendatore for so many years, found his subordinate position untenable, and in 1939 he left, bringing to a close his twenty-year career with Alfa Romeo.

Saying that he *left* Alfa Romeo in 1939 is a genteel way of saying he was fired. Ferrari began having repeated arguments with Gobbato over Ricard, and as Ferrari wrote, his heated discussions with Alfa's manager created a rift between them "that became unbridgeable and led to my dismissal. The crisis caused me to realize two things. Firstly, that I had been for too long a time with Alfa Romeo; and secondly, that when one is too long in an even indirect supervisory job, in the end the wear and tear inevitably begins to tell. I also came to the conclusion that to spend a whole lifetime with one firm was a mistake for anybody who wanted to learn: to learn, one must move about and do other jobs."

The interior of the 166 Barchetta features beautiful hand-sewn leather upholstery and trim. Its simplicity of design was purely race bred. The cars were considered luxurious, or *lusso*, when given the full interior treatment.

It was November 1939, and, after two decades with the same company most men would have taken their pensions and retired to a life of leisure, but at age forty-seven, Enzo Anselmo Ferrari had another idea; he sought a reaffirmation of his destiny. Rather than retire on the laurels of his brilliant career with Alfa Romeo, he embarked upon a new adventure as an independent industrialist, establishing a factory in Maranello, the Emilian town situated on the flat plain of the Po in the mountain chain of the Apennines some ten miles south of his birthplace in Modena.

Ferrari later described this decision to start anew: "My return to Modena after twenty years, in order to transform myself from a racing driver and team organizer into a small industrialist, marked not only the conclusion of what I might call an almost biological cycle, it represented also an attempt to prove to myself and to others that,

The sensuality of Ferrari was never more evident than in the first sports car, the Touring Barchetta. The ominous grille opening and hood scoop influenced automotive designs in Europe, Great Britain, and the United States well into the 1960s.

during the twenty years I was with Alfa Romeo, not all my reputation was second-hand and gained by the efforts of others. The time had come for me to see how far I could get by my own efforts."

Indeed, the accomplishments that had made Scuderia Ferrari renowned throughout European racing circles in the 1930s would serve to establish Enzo Ferrari as an automaker the moment word got out that he was going to build his own cars.

Ferrari named his new endeavor Auto Avio Costruzione. The first race car was built in 1939 in the old Scuderia Ferrari workshop in Modena. His first customers were Alberto Ascari and the Marchese Lotario Rangoni Machiavelli of Modena, who might be regarded as Ferrari's first patron. The eight-cylinder, 1.5-liter race car was designed by Alberto Massimino, who had also left Alfa Romeo's racing division. It was ready for the 1940 Grand Prix of Brescia, which was run in place of that year's Mille Miglia. The car, however, bore neither Ferrari's name nor the Scuderia Ferrari crest. Lamented Ferrari, "I was still bound by a clause [in the agreement signed with Alfa Romeo upon his departure] that forbade my reconstituting the

Scuderia Ferrari or engaging in motor racing activities for four years." Alfa Romeo management feared that the Ferrari name might be misconstrued as still part of the company's racing department. Thus, Ferrari's first race car was known simply as Model 815, indicating the number of cylinders and the engine capacity–eight cylinders, 1.5 liters.

As for the four-year noncompetition agreement, that was easily consumed by World War II, but by June 1945, a month after V-E Day, when Enzo was free to begin building cars under his own name, there were precious few customers with the liras to purchase one. Being on the losing side of the conflict had left Italy in a shambles both financially and, in some regions, where ground battles had been fought by Allied and German forces, quite literally. Ferrari had survived the war building machine tools for the military, and now, free to resume his automotive career, he was disillusioned by the dearth of patrons for handcrafted racing machines in Italy. Had it not been for the intervention of Luigi Chinetti, there might not have been a Ferrari legend to be written.

Luigi Chinetti, Sr., also worked for Alfa Romeo in the 1930s and had become a long-distance friend of Ferrari's after moving to the United States at the beginning of the war. He had accompanied the Ecurie Schell Maserati team and the

French race drivers Rene Dreyfus and Rene Le Begue to the United States, where they were going to compete in the 1939 Indianapolis 500. Chinetti had signed on as the team manager. When the war prevented him from returning to Europe, Chinetti decided to stay in the United States. And after the attack on Pearl Harbor, which drew America into the conflict, he decided to make New York his home and become an American citizen.

After the war, Chinetti, his wife, Marion, and young son, Luigi Jr., traveled to France, where they planned to vacation before going on to Italy. In Modena, Enzo Ferrari was struggling with the likelihood that he would never again build race cars. Chinetti heard of this, and on Christmas Eve 1946, the forty-five-year-old Italian race driver and automotive entrepreneur packed his wife and son into the car and drove to Modena. Rather than celebrating the holiday, he found Enzo sitting alone in his office, contemplating the future. He was at a crossroad, torn between an unfulfilling business and the need to return to what gave him pleasure—the design and production of race cars.

Luigi Chinetti, Jr., remembers that wintry Christmas as being like a scene from an Ingmar Bergman film. Though only a child at the time, he has never forgotten his first impression

The spare took up most of the Barchetta's trunk, and what was left was consumed by the fuel tank.

In 1952 Enzo Ferrari presented this 212 Touring Barchetta to Henry Ford II. The car's avant-garde styling may have contributed to the design of the 1955 Thunderbird. This car chassis 0253/EU was built on Ferrari's long 2,600 - millimeter (104-inch) wheelbase. The short wheelbase models had a length of only 2,200 millimeters (86.6 inches).

One element that remained consistent throughout the production of the Barchetta was the interior layout, a simple, functional design suited for racing. On the Ford car the steering was changed to the left side, almost unheard of for Ferrari sports and racing cars in 1952. The transmission was a five-speed used in most Ferrari models of the era.

of the imperious Enzo Ferrari sitting in his cold, dimly lit office, a single bare bulb hanging from the ceiling above his desk. In the frugality of the early postwar years, heating office buildings was almost unheard of, and the small room was so cold that, when Ferrari first spoke, his breath hovered in the air like fog.

Chinetti Sr. sat and explained to Ferrari that there was indeed a market for his race cars, not in Europe but in the United States. He then laid out a plan. "Let's make automobiles," he said. "That is the one thing we are good at." Ferrari considered the idea and spoke of hiring Gioacchino Colombo, another former Alfa Romeo colleague, to develop engines. That night Luigi Chinetti and Enzo Ferrari set into motion events that would lead to the postwar revitalization of Auto Avio Costruzione, soon to become Auto Costruzione Ferrari.

Of course, neither Ferrari nor Chinetti had the money to start a new business, but Chinetti had made many connections in the world

Head on it was 100 percent Ferrari in the bold styling idiom of the 1950s.

Carrozzeria Touring in Milan designed the original Barchetta body in 1948. The styling of the last Barchetta built for Henry Ford II in 1952 was quite different.

of motor sports and had wealthy friends both in France and in the United States, investors who could seed the start-up of manufacturing. Returning to New York, and with only gentleman's agreements in hand, he placed orders for the first eight cars. He then told Ferrari that he could sell twenty-five cars. And he did, many through the newly organized Chinetti Motors in Manhattan, which became the exclusive importer for Ferrari automobiles and parts in the United States.

In creating his first postwar sports cars, Ferrari decided that if Maserati built four-cylinder engines, Talbot six, and Alfa Romeo eight, he would build a twelve. It was a resolution that the Ferrari historian Hans Tanner would later refer to as "daring and farsighted."

On May 11, 1947, the very first car bearing the Ferrari name appeared in public in Italy. Sports cars were practicing for racing at Piacenza, and two versions of the new Ferrari Tipo 125 S 1.5-liter sports car were shown—a simple, two-seat Spyder Corsa, later referred to in an Italian newspaper as "small, red and ugly," and a roadster with full body work by Carrozzeria Touring Superleggera. The 125 S was powered by a sixty-degree V12 engine designed, as Ferrari had suggested that first night in December 1946, by Gioacchino Colombo.

By 1948, the Ferrari factory was producing a small number of twelve-cylinder competition models. One of the earliest examples to wear the yellow and black Cavallino Rampante emblem was the

The Superleggera hood emblem indicated that the car was of Carrozzeria Touring's exclusive lightweight construction. The Superleggera name became as well recognized as that of the Milanese coachbuilder.

Tipo 166 Spyder Corsa, a simple, cycle-fendered version very similar in appearance to the previous year's Type 125 S and 159 S. That any resemblance to a road car could be found surrounding any early Ferrari chassis was a tribute to the Milanese firm of Touring.

One of Italy's oldest design houses, Touring was established in 1926 by Carlo Felice Bianchi Anderloni, renowned for designing and building some of the most exciting sports cars of the 1930s. Enzo Ferrari's relationship with Touring dated back to the years when he had managed the Scuderia, and Anderloni designed and produced the majority of bodies for the Alfa factory's racing cars.

Convinced by Chinetti of the necessity to offer models with more cosmopolitan appeal to serve the needs of both road and

Bold dual air intakes atop the hood were among the styling cues shown on the last Barchetta.

Although the Ford car was built on the Tipo 212 platform, the engine was the new 2,562-cubic-centimeter Colombo V12 used in the 225 S race cars. The design used a single overhead camshaft, two distributors, wet sump lubrication, and a trio of 36DCF Weber carburetors.

The Ford Barchetta was fitted with Borrani 5.90 x 15 wire-spoke wheels. Henry Ford II had the Borrani wheels reshod with one-off Firestone 500 whitewall racing tires, which appealed to him more than the black Pirelli racing tires the car had come with.

track, Ferrari retained Anderloni to create sports car bodies, this time to complement the unattractive but successful cycle-fendered Spyder Corsas that had become standard Ferrari fare. A year later the first sports car design ever shown on a Ferrari chassis, the 166 MM Touring Barchetta, was introduced. Few cars have left such a lasting impression on the motoring world.

More than half a century after its debut, it is still among the most admired of all Ferrari models. The styling of the Barchetta was based in part on the BMW 328 Spyder designed by Carrozzeria Touring in 1940. All the Barchetta bodies, of which Touring built some forty-six examples, shared the same sleek, swept-back lines, long hood, short rear deck, and aggressively shaped oval grille, establishing this feature as a Ferrari trait for years to come. Those very descriptive words, "long hood, short rear deck," would be heard echoing from the halls of Detroit automakers in the 1960s and would be used by Lee Iacocca to describe the benchmark 1964-$\frac{1}{2}$ Ford Mustang!

The Barchetta's visceral styling would also inspire the Tojiero Specials in England and the AC Ace and AC Bristol, which evolved into the Shelby Cobras of the 1960s. In one bold stroke, Ferrari and Anderloni had ingeniously closed the distance between race car and road car without compromising either.

Anderloni wrote that the styling of the Barchetta was both a fascinating and a courageous undertaking: It was "fascinating because we were attempting to individualize the Ferrari and not to copy one of the many 'Spider' two-seat sports cars in circulation. Courageous because the results were obtained by overturning the strictest canons of sports car design, which was normally wide at the bottom, narrow at the top, and close to the ground." The Barchetta had its maximum width just over halfway up the side and visibly high off the ground. It was so different from other sports cars, said Anderloni, that when journalists saw it on the Ferrari stand at the 1948 Turin Salon, they found it necessary to nickname the design Barchetta, which means "small boat" in Italian, and from that moment on the new Ferrari body style was distinguished from all other two-seat sports cars. Officially, the cars were cataloged as the 166 Mille Miglia or 166 MM, a name chosen in honor of Ferrari's 1948 victory in the grueling thou-

sand-mile Italian road race; Barchetta, however, was readily used by everyone, even Ferrari.

The Touring design was revolutionary not only in form, utilizing the firm's exclusive Superleggera or superlight construction method of small, lightweight steel tubes to which the body panels were attached, but in color scheme, sheathed in a unique blend of slightly metallicized red, not an orange red or a lipstick red but a color unique to Ferrari. Most of the 166 MMs were painted this deep, fiery hue, which has become another Ferrari tradition. Virtually every Barchetta was a race car, whether a competition model powered by the 140-horsepower Export V12, or the more luxurious Lusso, with the 110-horsepower Inter V12.

The front-end treatment was somewhat different from the original Barchetta design, but the rear styling was a total departure with a unique fender and taillight design. Interestingly, this car was built before either the 1955 Thunderbird or the 1953 Corvette!

Another engine variation seen with the Barchetta body was the Tipo 195 S. This was produced in 1950 and displaced 2,341 cubic centimeters from a bore x stroke of 65 x 58.8 millimeters. Output was 160 horsepower at 7,000 revolutions per minute. The engine's designation was based on the displacement of each cylinder, i.e., 195.1 cubic centimeters.

The Barchetta's hand-built body was attached to a welded tubular steel framework and then mounted on Ferrari's short 2,200-millimeter (86.6-inch) wheelbase. The front suspension was Ferrari's independent A-arm design, supported by a single transverse leaf spring; the rear, a live axle with semielliptic springs and parallel trailing arms on each side. Early Ferraris also used Houdaille hydraulic-lever-action type dampers.

The 166 Mille Miglia was arguably the fastest sports car in the world at the time, and with it Ferrari's cannonade across Europe recorded more than eighty overall or class victories between April 1948 and December 1953. Enzo Ferrari had handily reclaimed his racing reputation.

In March 1949, Clemente Biondetti won the Targa Florio in a 166 MM, and 166 Inters were first and second in the Coppa Inter-Europa.

In April, Biondetti and Felice Bonetto, driving 166 MMs, finished first and second in the Mille Miglia. But it was Luigi Chinetti who brought Ferrari its greatest victory, codriving a 166 MM Touring Barchetta with Britain's Lord Peter Selsdon in the 1949 Vingt-quatre Heures du Mans. At nearly fifty years of age, "Iron Man Chinetti" drove twenty-three of the twenty-four hours to clinch Ferrari's first and most important international win. He went on to win the Spa-Francorchamps twenty-four-hour race for touring cars the following July. In 1950, Alberto Ascari won the Grand Prix du Luxembourg and the Silverstone International Trophy. Dorino Serafini and Luigi Villoresi came in second at Silverstone, driving a single-carburetor Barchetta, in all probability the very car pictured in this book, which was sold to Chinetti and later to the American race driver Bill Spear.

For the longest time thereafter, whenever the name Ferrari was mentioned, people would immediately picture the 166 MM Barchetta, the first and perhaps the most charismatic of all early Ferrari sports cars.

The very last Barchetta body was built by Touring in 1952 and fitted to a 212 chassis. It was given as a gift by Enzo Ferrari to Henry Ford II and delivered new with the larger 225 (2,715-cubic-centimeter) engine used in the 225S race cars. Unusual for the era, Ford's car was also equipped with left-hand drive. The American automaker later fitted the black Ferrari with a one-off set of Firestone 500 whitewall racing tires, replacing the standard and less fashionable black 6.50-15 Pirellis.

The design of this car, chassis 0253/EU, was the most avant-garde of all the Barchetta bodies produced by Carrozzeria Touring and defined a number of styling cues that were later seen in the final version of the groundbreaking 1955 Ford Thunderbird. One can also see a hint of 1953 Corvette in the car's coachwork lines, particularly in the rear quarters.

"At FoMoCo," wrote the Barchetta's third owner, the former Ford and later GM styling, product planning, and research executive Dick Merritt, "the car was 'off limits' and only one or two top executives were even allowed to drive it. The styling people studied it for ideas at the time they were designing the Thunderbird. It was measured thoroughly, but I'm sure the engineers never ran any tests, or took it apart as they usually do." Well, almost.

During the summer of 1955, as it was later reported, a Ford test driver named Ted Mullee, "working midnights," discovered Henry Ford's Ferrari in the garage, where it was undergoing an exhaust repair. "Not knowing there were only exhaust headers on the vehicle," wrote the *Prancing Horse* editor Howard Payne, "he pushed the vehicle out of the garage and out to the test track, while all of the other drivers were at lunch. Once on the track entrance ramp (2:30 A.M.), Tom fired up the Ferrari; yes he did let it warm up, then he was off on his midnight ride. I cannot imagine the thrill young Tom Mullee felt on a warm, moonlit summer night in an open Ferrari, with no exhaust restraints, on the high speed loop of the Ford test track."

In 1949 Luigi Chinetti, Sr., won the 24 Hours of Le Mans driving a 166 MM. Giving Ferrari its first significant victory on foreign soil, Chinetti (pictured with Selsdon at far right) drove twenty-three of the twenty-four hours, with Britain's Lord Peter Selsdon clocking only one hour behind the wheel.

Unfortunately for Mullee, the roar of the Ferrari's unrestrained 2.7-liter, triple-carbureted 225S racing engine awoke just about everyone staying at the posh Dearborn Inn, just across the street from the test track! When he exited the track after seven or eight hot laps, he was met by the track manager and the rest of the test crew. He got three days off without pay for his indiscretion, but even years later Mullee reminisced about that night and claimed it was worth it. Such was the allure of the car Enzo Ferrari gave to Henry Ford II.

The historian and author Phil Skinner, who knew Merritt, recalls that Merritt was hired by Ford on November 18, 1956, to be a product planner for the Special Products Division, which at the time was developing a new line of cars then known as the E-car. He would become one of the shortest-term employees of the Special Products Division, for the very next day, November 19, 1956, the announcement came down that the new line of cars would be the Edsel, and those working on the project would now be working for the Edsel Division of Ford Motor Company.

As he related the story to Skinner, Merritt was already a fan of the Ferrari; its performance, styling, and engineering were all cutting edge for the day. Now this was Merritt's very first job in the auto industry after graduating from college, and he was a little bit wet behind the ears. No one told him part of the etiquette at Ford World Headquarters was that you only spoke to Mr. Ford if he directed a question to you. One fateful day, he spotted Henry II walking down the hall with several of his associates on the way to a meeting. Knowing that this might be his only opportunity, he walked up to Henry Ford II and blurted out, "Mr. Ford, I really think that Ferrari of yours

is really sharp. Would you let me know when you're ready to sell it?"

Now, we are talking about a guy who maybe was earning $3,600 a year, talking to a man worth millions about a car that cost $10,000 when new and had a market value then of at least $6,000 to $7,000. Reportedly Henry Ford II was taken aback by this upstart kid, gave him a somewhat semicourteous nod, and moved on to his appointed rounds.

It would be several months later that Merritt got the chance to own the car. He had a little difficulty convincing the bank to lend him more than a year's wages to buy a car, and a used one at that. The price, though, was spectacular, just $4,000, and his argument was that the car listed for $10,000 just a few years ago, and new ones cost even more! He swung the loan, lived very lean for awhile, but owned one of the most impressive and sharpest-looking cars ever to bear the Ferrari name.

Stirling Moss summarized Enzo's life in several paragraphs that composed the foreword of Ferrari's 1963 memoirs, *My Terrible Joys*. Wrote Sir Stirling, "To nearly every motoring enthusiast the name Ferrari means, and has meant for some years, the essence of motoring in the truly grand manner: the art and science of automobile engineering at its greatest." That was an opinion shared by virtually every sports and race car enthusiast in 1965, and it is still true more than forty years later.

Chapter 3

Early Road and Race Cars—Building an Image on Road and Track

When two stubborn men are at odds, little is ever accomplished, but when they work together, the results are often astounding. Such were the good days that Chinetti and Ferrari shared.

The difference between Ferrari's race cars and road cars in the early postwar era was solely a matter of interpretation. The race cars could, for the most part, be driven on the road, and the handful of road cars produced were also suitable for racing. But, like the visually stunning Barchetta, they were far from practical cars, strictly fair-weather automobiles with no tops and with unadorned interiors devoid of comfort or convenience features. Chinetti explained to Ferrari that what he needed for the road was a cabriolet. Ferrari commissioned Stabilimenti Farina to design and build the very first such car on chassis 011 S.

In 1949, at the famed Geneva Salon, the very first Ferrari convertible made its debut with Luigi Chinetti at its side. This was the first time a Ferrari had been exhibited to the public outside Italy. With the obvious exception of the roof, and a flatter trunk, made necessary by the cabriolet top, the convertible's design was almost identical to the 166 coupe. The body lines were simple, which was typical of Italian designs. Aside

Stabilimenti Farina produced the first Ferrari cabriolet (011 S), pictured here. This is one of the oldest known of the road cars, built in 1949 and displayed at the Geneva Salon by Luigi Chinetti. Geneva was Ferrari's first showing outside Italy. The lines of the car were similar to those of other Farina and Pinin Farina designs of the time, such as the Alfa Romeo 6C 2500, and were repeated on the Simca Sport.

from the grille and bumpers, this first Ferrari cabriolet resembled the early postwar Alfa Romeo 6C 2500 Sport, designed by Pinin Farina, and the basic body lines of both cars were not too distant from those of the 1947 Cisitalia. The prototype cabriolet was later purchased by the Italian film director Roberto Rossellini. Farina produced several subsequent cabriolets through 1950, though no two were alike.

One of the significant turning points in Ferrari road car production came in 1951, with the introduction of the Tipo 212. The 212 Berlinetta marked the beginning of a new era in Maranello. Whereas racing had once been Enzo Ferrari's sole raison d'être, the design and production of road cars had now become of equal importance. Chinetti had finally convinced Enzo that not everyone enthralled by reverie of the Ferrari's V12 and exhilarating performance wanted to race, or to suffer the discomfort of a race car's purposeful interior and cockpit.

The Farina cabriolet (011 S) was among the first to cross the line that had been so firmly drawn by Enzo Ferrari, and the first open car to offer a convertible top. The idea of producing an open Ferrari that was not a *competizione* came from Luigi Chinetti. The basic body lines of this Ferrari cabriolet were nearly identical to those of the Stabilimenti Farina coupe. With the top raised, the 166 became an all-weather sports car. It was the beginning of a new era for Ferrari.

The identification plate shows that the first Ferrari cabriolet was a 166 Inter. The 011 S car is in original condition, although at some point in its history it was repainted from the light color shown in 1949 to its present shade of deep red.

Top right: Instruments are large Jaeger design with the Ferrari logo imprinted. The dashboard and instrument panel is painted metal.

Although Ferrari considered competition his first priority and had little, if any, interest in building cars for nonracing clientele, Chinetti convinced him that one could serve the needs of the other. Chinetti's logic was sound. Improvements in race car design enhanced the road cars, and the profits from road car sales financed the development of still better race cars. Ferrari's racing engines could be detuned for the street, and, as for coachwork, in postwar Italy there was no shortage of carrozziera available to clothe Ferrari's magnificent chassis. This bespoke coachwork graced a number of early cars, exquisite two- and four-place creations such as Touring's 166 Inter coupe, the Ghia 212 Inter, and Pinin Farina's breathtaking Tipo 342 America of 1953. But these were all extremely limited, handcrafted cars. In later years, Enzo finally came around to Chinetti's way of

Beneath the elegantly shaped hood was a V12 utilizing a single carburetor, a unique two-part air filter, and special covers integrating the ignition, all characteristics of the first touring Ferrari models. This is the original engine from the 166 Inter, bodied by Stabilimenti Farina for the 1949 Geneva Salon.

thinking, remarking that he now had three main categories of clientele: "the sportsman, the fifty-year-olds, and the exhibitionists."

Among the most stylish of early Ferrari road cars were those built by Carrozzeria Vignale. The luxurious Vignale 212 Inter was intended as a touring car but also managed to acquit itself quite well when pressed into competition. A pair of 212 Inters finished first and second in the 1951 Carrera PanAmericana, with Piero Taruffi and Luigi Chinetti in the lead car, and Alberto Ascari and Luigi Villoresi close behind. The 212 could also be ordered in a stripped-down Export or *competizione* version. Even when built for racing, the Vignale was a car with striking savoir faire. In all, it is estimated, and only estimated, since the assignment of serial numbers in the early years was less than precise, that around eighty Tipo 212 Inter (noncompe-

tition models) and twenty-seven Export (racing) versions were built.

The Vignale 212 Inter represents the quintessence of the Italian coachbuilder's art in the 1950s. And it is here that the true romance of Ferrari's early years can be seen. The beauty of the Vignale lies in the intricate detail of each and every facet of design. There is so much handwork that one must study even the smallest appointments to appreciate the craftsmanship that went into the cars: hand-tooled door pulls with small Vignale cloisonné emblems, chromed window moldings and trim work, hand-sewn leather and fabrics. In virtually every detail, inside and out, this was the work of artisans.

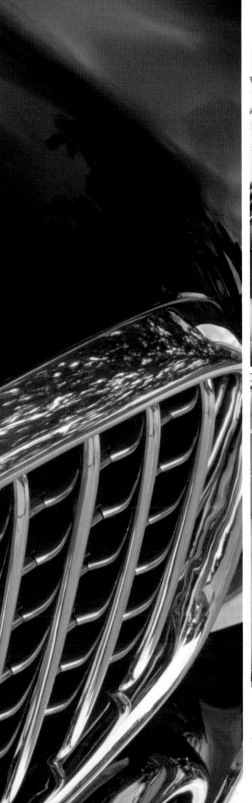

This page:
As production of Ferrari road cars progressed, interior treatments became more luxurious and leather to cover door panels and the transmission tunnel more common. Aside from the instruments and the basic outline of the dashboard, interior decor was at the discretion of the coachbuilder and the client.

Far left:
One of the most prominent styling characteristics of the Pinin Farina design on chassis 0117 E was the grille and forward air intake, both profusely embellished with chrome.

The engine for the 212 Inter was of 2,562.51 cubic centimeters (156.3 cubic inches) in displacement, fueled by three Weber 36DCF carburetors. Output was rated at 180 horsepower at 7,000 revolutions per minute, with 8:1 compression. (Other figures show 170 horsepower at 6,500 rpm.) Earlier engines had one 36 DCF Weber twin-choke carburetor and developed 130 horsepower at 6,000 rpm. The original Colombo sixty-degree V12 was fitted with light-alloy cylinder head and block, special cast-iron pressed-in liners, an increased bore of 68 millimeters (2.68 inches), and the standard stroke of 58.8 millimeters (2.315 inches). Power was delivered via a five-speed crash box with direct drive in fourth gear.

A handsome Farina cloisonné was placed at the center of the deck lid handle. The emblem was also placed on the front fenders with the *Pinin Farina* in chrome beneath.

Among the more striking designs on the 212 Inter was the very first collaboration between Ferrari and Pinin Farina, a cabriolet on chassis 0117 E delivered June 17, 1952. It was a low-line two-seater distinguished by a grille of generous dimensions, a hood with double air intakes, and a sweeping, integrated fender line that combined a subtle but distinctive return of the taillight pod into the rear fender.

One of the car's most significant details was actually a lack of detail; the body was flat sided, interrupted only by the wheel arches, a most unusual design trait in the early 1950s.

The distinction between road car and race car was still of little consequence, and several of Ferrari's most alluring *competizione* also made superb Berlinetta and Spyder versions for the road. Of the latter, the short-lived Tipo 225 S stands out as one of Maranello's most intriguing dual-purpose models. How then did one distinguish between a Ferrari race car and a Ferrari sports car in the early 1950s? If Piero Taruffi or Alberto Ascari was driving, it was a race car.

Between 1948 and 1952, Ferrari continued to increase the swept volume of his twelve-cylinder engines, with each succeeding version more fortunate in competition than the last, and each with increasingly attractive coachwork by Touring, Pinin Farina, and Vignale.

The 212 chassis measured 2,250 millimeters (88.6 inches) with front and rear tracks of 1,270 millimeters (49.8 inches) and 1,250 millimeters (49.2 inches), respectively. Coachwork varied from builder to builder, with Vignale, perhaps only in the shadow of Pinin Farina, producing the most stirring designs of all. A number of 212 Inter and Export coupes were, in a word, unflattering. Those from Vignale were usually striking in appearance and anticipated designs that would appear elsewhere. The similarities between the 1951 Vignale coupe, pictured, and the much coveted 340 Mexico are unmistakable.

With sports cars continually profiting from the lessons of the race track, the outcome was often an interim model, such as the 225 S. While the Barchetta would become the most popular Ferrari body style on the Tipos 166, 195 S, and 212 chassis, the 225 S was by far the most exciting open car of its day. A listing of serial numbers shows that about twenty were built during the model's single year of production, 1952, and that all but one had coachwork by Vignale: twelve Spyder and seven Berlinetta bodies. Of those, around half a dozen had the *Tuboscocca* form of chassis-frame with double outer tubes, one above the other, joined by a trusslike arrangement, with additional tubing used to create a skeleton outline of the body shape, to which hand-formed panels could be fitted.

Luxurious interior detail of the 212 Inter by Vignale featured leather upholstery and plush carpet throughout. There is so much hand labor that one must study even the smallest appointments to appreciate the workmanship that went into the Vignale cars.

Top left: The standard door latch for the Ferrari 212 was a recessed handle actuated by pressing the lock button. This is the same basic design that would later appear on the Mercedes-Benz 300 SL production cars.

Bottom left and right: A hybrid of the 212 Inter and the Export, this luxurious Vignale coupe was equipped with competition gas tank and fuel filler, and an exposed spare wheel, but with the luxurious trim and upholstery of the Lusso model. This example, chassis 175 E, is believed, though not documented, to have competed in the 1951 Carrera PanAmericana.

Tucked neatly under the Vignale 212's hood is a 2,562-cubic-centimeter, sixty-degree V12 delivering 170 horsepower.

The 1952 Type 225 S pictured, chassis number 0160 ED, was driven for Scuderia Ferrari in the 1952 Tour of Sicily by Piero Taruffi. The second Vignale sports racing Spyder built, 0160 ED featured the traditional styling used on most of the 2.7-liter cars, including the distinctive ovoid ports cut into the front fenders. Among the most significant styling cues of the 225 S, these ports were not part of the original concept. They were added by Vignale following the Tour of Sicily to improve ventilation of the engine compartment. At the same time, Vignale removed the car's running lights ,and the round openings that had flanked the oval grille were converted to air intakes, creating a new, more aggressive front visage that would be reprised on the Vignale-bodied 250 MM and 340 MM Ferraris.

The interior of the 225 S was nothing exciting, but, as with all Vignale designs, even a simple instrument panel had an air of elegance. In this instance, the two large combination gauges were positioned on the dash in a slightly flared and lowered center fascia. The panel was accented with a bold Vignale emblem.

Opposite:
A trio of 36DCF Weber carburetors delivered the air-fuel mix to the V12 engine in the 225 Sport. With an 8.5:1 compression ratio, output was 210 horsepower at 7,200 revolutions per minute discharged to the rear wheels via a five-speed gearbox integral with the engine. The capacity of the Colombo short-block was increased to 2,715 cubic centimeters by taking the bore out to 70 millimeters. While the engine remained basically Colombo, the roller cam followers introduced by Lampredi were used. Most engines also had twelve port heads.

The 225 Sport followed the design of the 212 Inter, with a Colombo short-block V12, bored and stroked to 70.0 millimeters x 58.8 millimeters, and a cubic capacity of 2.7 liters.

Essentially an engine variation, the 225 S shared the 212's chassis, with double wishbone, transleaf spring front, and rigid axle, semi-elliptic spring rear suspension, and the same physical dimensions: a wheelbase of 2,250 millimeters (88.6 inches) with front and rear tracks of 1,278 millimeters (50.4 inches) and 1,250 millimeters (49.25 inches) respectively. The only notable difference was that the 225 S used 5.25 x 16 tires on the front, compared with the 212's 5.50 x 16. Rear tires were identical at 6.50 x 16. It was the car's styling, more than anything else, that set it apart from other Ferrari of the period.

Drivers and engineers always surrounded Ferrari (second from left). Here he is flanked by driver Alberto Ascari (far left), racing department director Federico Giberti, and chief engineer Aurelio Lampredi (far right). The photo was taken at the Grand Prix of Italy in February 1950.

A 212 Export Berlinetta, bodied by Vignale, won the 1951 Coppa Inter-Europa with driver Luigi Villoresi.

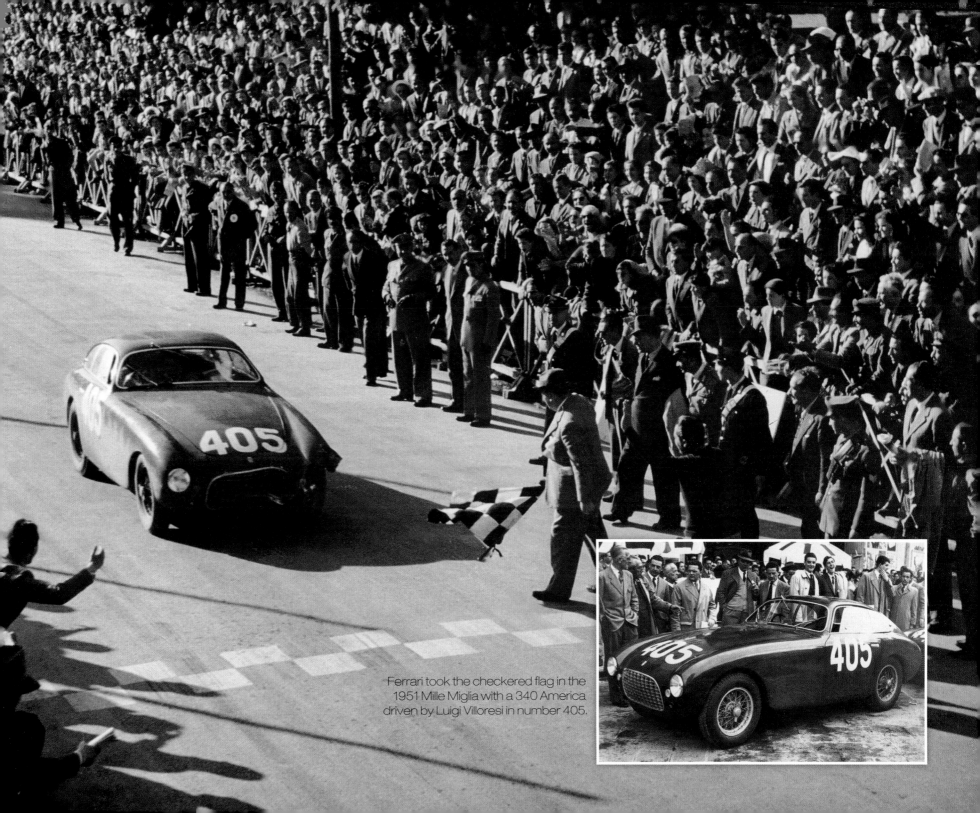

Ferrari took the checkered flag in the 1951 Mille Miglia with a 340 America driven by Luigi Villoresi in number 405.

In the 1952 Mille Miglia, Ferraris lined the street at the start. At the front of the queue is a Ferrari 340 America; behind it is the 250 S that won the race, with driver Giovanni Bracco beating a Mercedes-Benz 300 SL in the only event that year not won by the Mercedes team.

Bracco's car, number 611, makes a photo finish just minutes ahead of the second place Mercedes-Benz 300 SL.

In May 1952 the car pictured, originally driven for Ferrari by Piero Taruffi, was sold through a dealer in Rome to Roberto Bonami, who campaigned the 225 Sport throughout South America, winning the 1953 Buenos Aires 1000km race and the Argentine Sports Car Championship in both 1952 and 1953. Two years later, on January 23, 1955, this same car finished sixth overall in the 1000km of Buenos Aires. It has led what most would call a charmed life—never crashed, never abused, still with its original engine, and in good hands from the day it was built. It is a far cry from that first "small, red and ugly" Ferrari.

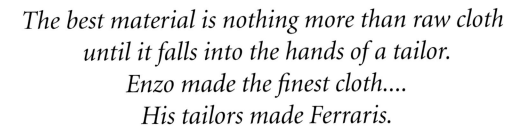

The best material is nothing more than raw cloth until it falls into the hands of a tailor.
Enzo made the finest cloth....
His tailors made Ferraris.

By the mid-1950s, Ferrari was primarily relying on Pinin Farina and Vignale to design and produce a substantial number of road cars. Carrozzeria Vignale catered to a number of prominent postwar Italian automakers, including Ferrari, but, compared with Touring and Pinin Farina it was a relatively new company. The Vignale brothers had established their small workshop in Turin's Grugliasco district in 1939, but it was not until after the war that Vignale became successful. In the early postwar years, Alfredo Vignale attracted a number of his former workmates away from the big Pinin Farina concern, establishing his carrozzeria as a small, more contemporary design house. Vignale later moved to a new facility in Turin and took in a partner, Angelo Balma, and a promising young designer named Giovanni Michelotti. Within two years, Carrozzeria Vignale had become a recognized car body designer, and through the firm's work for Ferrari in the early 1950s, it rose to international fame. From 1950 to 1953, the Vignale works produced bodies for Ferrari that won three Mille Miglia and one Carrera PanAmericana.

The 410 Superamerica was a road car in the fullest sense, as its size and weight, an average of 3,500 pounds, would have given it a decided handicap in racing. The handling and ride characteristics of the 410 Superamerica were better suited to vast open highways and cross-country touring than to winding mountain roads and city traffic. Given a good stretch of blacktop, the 4.9-liter V12 could propell the 410 well into the triple digits.

Ferrari's road cars were composed of the 212 series, which was discontinued in 1953 and overlapped with the short-lived 340 America, 342 America, and 375 America, introduced in 1953. These were the first Ferrari road cars to gain a foothold in the United States, where, by the early 1950s, Luigi Chinetti had established Ferrari as the most prestigious line of imported sports and racing cars.

Chinetti had some pretty tough competition, sharing the New York spotlight with the automotive importer and entrepreneur Max Hoffman, who had a plush showroom designed by Frank Lloyd Wright in the heart of New York City. Hoffman offered a selection of stunning new sports cars from Porsche, BMW, and Mercedes-Benz, including the 1954 300 SL Gullwing Coupe, the automotive scion of the world-beating 1952 Mercedes-Benz 300 SL race cars. Like Chinetti, Hoffman had the pulse of America's sports car elite, and the battle for sales was fought all the way from the showroom floor to the pits at Watkins Glen and the Pebble Beach road races in California. But Chinetti had something Hoffman didn't. He had Ferrari.

Opposite:
The Pinin Farina design for the 410 Superamerica surrounded Ferrari's bold oval grille with high crowned fenders stretched into one fluid line along the length of the body and into a pronounced kickup just behind the doors.

The car's elegant profile was accentuated by a wraparound backlight, slightly finned rear fenders, and a distinctive rear fender cleave that swept downward to the rockers, creating a sweep panel effect from the doors forward. Like the 340 and 375 America before it, the 410 was designed with the American market in mind. The master of design, Sergio Pininfarina, photographed by the author in 1981, when Pininfarina opened the Carrozzeria Italiana exhibit at the Pasadena Conference Center, in Pasadena, California. Explained Pininfarina: "It is not a matter of styling the car in one way more than another but designing the right type of car for the [American] market."

When the 410 Superamerica was unveiled in 1956, it became the first Ferrari road car intended to be sold in North America. It came on the heels of a short series of interim models beginning with the 340 America, a car that proved moderately successful, although of the twenty-two constructed, only eight were even discernible as road cars. The 340 was followed in the winter of 1952–53 by the more luxurious 342 America, the first road car offered with left-hand drive. All Ferrari models before the 342 America were right-hand drive,

just like the factory race cars! It wasn't until production of the last 212 models that a left-hand drive Ferrari had even been considered. The 342 series was also short-lived, concluded after only six examples. It was a stopgap between the 340 America and the new, more powerful 375 America.

The 375 had its engine capacity increased to 4.5 liters (4,522.94 cubic centimeters or 275.8 cubic inches) with a bore x stroke of 84 millimeters x 68 millimeters (3.307 inches x 2.68 inches) and three twin-choke

The interior of the 410 Superamerica was more finely detailed than that of any previous Ferrari model. The car utilized a four-speed synchronized (Porsche-type) transmission but with different gear ratios from the 375 America. The most disconcerting feature of the transmission was that, on the majority of cars, first gear was found forward and to the right, and fourth was back and to the left.

42DCZ Webers replacing the 40DCF used on the 342. This new, more powerful model had been designed principally for Chinetti's North American clientele, whereas the companion 250 Europa, also introduced in 1953, was intended for the European market. Both models were unveiled at the Paris Motor Show in October and with the exception of engines, were almost identical. The Europa was fitted with a smaller, 3-liter V12. Production of the 375 America ended a year later, after approximately thirteen cars were built, the majority of which were bodied as coupes by Pinin Farina. With such limited production numbers, it is easy to understand the high values placed today on so many early Ferrari models.

In Detroit the construction of handcrafted cars was fast becoming a thing of the past by the early 1950s, and in Europe the introduction of unit-body construction after the war was further diminishing the demand and capacity for producing bespoke coachwork. Ferrari was an exception, still building cars in the manner of a decade before, delivering rolling chassis to the local

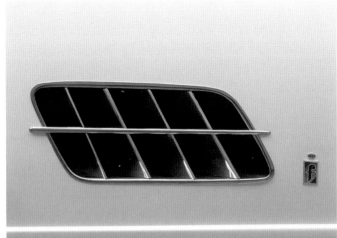

carrozziera to be individually bodied. In the very early postwar years, Ferrari relied on Carrozzeria Touring and Stabilimenti Farina.

Farina, which opened its doors in 1905, was one of the oldest body builders in Turin. From the house of Farina came talented designers such as Mario Boano, Giovanni Michelotti, and, of course, the youngest Farina brother, Battista "Pinin" Farina, who established his own atelier in 1930. Two decades later, Pinin Farina took over the work of Stabilimenti Farina and, with his son Sergio, began working closely with Maranello to design coachwork equal to the expectations of Ferrari's wealthy clientele.

Recalls Sergio Pininfarina: "After the war, in 1947, my father designed the best car he ever did, the Cisitalia. I think it set the pace for the design of sports cars throughout the next decade. Indeed, it is virtually impossible to look at any European sports car designed in the 1950s and fail to see some resemblance to the Cisitalia. As I look at it today it is still so simple, so

The 4.9-liter V12 engine was similar to the ones employed on the 1951 Formula One and on all sports cars until 1954. Displacement, however, was brought to the 5-liter limit through the use of new liners. The Lampredi-designed long-block sixty-degree V12 displaced 4,961.57 cubic centimeters (302.7 cubic inches) with an 88 x 68 millimeter (3.46 x 2.68 inch) bore x stroke, 8.5:1 compression ratio, and an output of 340 horsepower at 6,000 revolutions per minute.

The 375 MM was a purebred race car. This 1954 example is shown in competition with driver Jocky Maasland.

Left: The 250 MM, this example from 1953, was driven to victory by Luigi Villoresi in the Grand Prix at Monza.

Right: Enzo Ferrari (left) poses with the great Italian designer Battista Pinin Farina in front of the 250 MM at Monza.

The 250 MM's wheelbase measured 2,400 millimeters (94.5 inches), the shortest Ferrari had built since the 212 Export at 2,250 millimeters (88.6 inches) and the 166 MM at 2,200 millimeters (86.6 inches). The example pictured is one of the most distinctive of the Vignale Spyders. Car 0332 MM was completed in early April 1953 as the ninth of twelve Vignales. The Spyder was originally delivered to the Scuderia Ferrari factory team and remains the only 250 MM Spyder to have such distinction. While each 250 MM varied in appearance, the 0332 MM was highly distinguished by Vignale's use of faired-in headlights, an aggressive front-leaning stance, and foreshortened front fenders. Notable Vignale traits were also the fender ports, triangular vents in the rear fenders, and air ducts in the rocker panels. This car competed in a total of twenty-five races from April 1953 to April 1956, beginning with the '53 Mille Miglia (fifth in class, ninth overall). The car's competition record includes five victories and four second-place finishes.

The cockpit of the 250 MM was just that, a place for the *pilota*, a traditional right-hand-drive racing configuration with two large combination gauges, bucket-type seats, and a large, wood-rimmed steering wheel. The 250 MM was equipped with a new four-speed all-synchromesh transmission.

well proportioned, a masterpiece, difficult to add anything to."

The 1950s was an important period for the Pinin Farina factory as it began to work with Ferrari. Sergio Pininfarina says, "In Italy, I would say we began to work with all the automobile manufacturers, and in Europe, with Peugeot, in England, British Leyland, and some Japanese firms. My father was also the first Italian to design an American-built car, the Nash Ambassador," adds Sergio with a note of pride. But it was Enzo Ferrari who brought the most prominence to Pinin Farina, not for the volume of work Maranello provided but rather because of the adulation each new design received from sports car cognoscenti the world over. Pininfarina has designed almost every Ferrari road car produced in the last fifty years.

Explains Sergio, "My inclination for sports cars is understood when you realize that when I was twenty-five years old, in 1951, my father gave me responsibility of the Ferrari section. Can you imagine a young engineer being responsible for the relation with Mr. Ferrari? He

was a difficult man, a great man, a man that, with my father, gave me my point of reference for the love and dedication to automobiles."

Although Pinin Farina had created several significant cars for Ferrari by 1956, the design of the 410 Superamerica was perhaps the most significant. Only nine examples of the 410 Superamerica were produced by Pinin Farina in this original style, but the styling cues created for it were carried on for nearly a decade. Discussing the original 410 Superamerica design, Sergio Pininfarina says, "It [was] not a matter of styling the car in one way more than another but designing the right type of car for the [American] market. The car is not always moving, and it must be something that the driver enjoys just looking at. And then people, ordinary people on the street, look at the car also, and they must see something special. It must have a definite personality that shows to the public distinctively that this is a Ferrari."

Car 0423 SA, trimmed in white with a contrasting black roof, graced the Ferrari stand at the Brussels Auto Show in February 1956. The

410 Superamerica turned more than a few heads, and its styling would become the foundation for the 250 GT PF coupes and the later 250 GT Berlinetta Tour de France design, and would strongly influence the 250 GT Cabriolet and Spyder California, with its distinctive rear fender kickup.

The 410 Superamerica had replaced the 375 America both mechanically and aesthetically, the America still bearing the heavier, rounded coachwork of early Ferrari road cars, such as the first Tour de France models, and other examples bodied by Pinin Farina, Vignale, Touring, and Carrozzeria Ghia.

Preceding the 410 Superamerica was a 375 concept car displayed at the Turin Motor Show in 1955. The styling of this sensational coupe, also in white with contrasting black roof, clearly predicted the body lines and color scheme of Pinin Farina's forthcoming 410 Superamerica. The renowned Ferrari historian Antoine Prunet wrote that the 410 "represented important progress in the design of the engine, the chassis, and the body."

As a bare chassis and engine displaying Ferrari's latest developments, the 410 Superamerica was shown at the Paris Motor Show in October 1955, and the following February it returned, clothed with the spectacular Pinin Farina body. The 410 utilized many of the same components along with the successful Lampredi-designed V12 engine that had won the Vingt-quatre Heures du Mans, the Buenos Aires 1000km, and the PanAmerican road

The competition V12 engine in this 250 MM delivered 240 horsepower at 7,200 revolutions per minute from a swept volume of 2,953 cubic centimeters (78 x 58.8 millimeters). The engine used one spark plug per cylinder and three Weber 36 IF4/C four-choke carburetors.

race. Noted Enzo, "Lampredi was undoubtedly the most prolific designer Ferrari ever had: starting from the 1-1/2 liter, 12-cylinder, he first produced the 3-liter, then the 3,750cc, then the 4-liter; these were followed by 4,200cc, the 4-1/2 liter and 4,900cc; all 12-cylinder engines."

The Lampredi V12 for the 410, increased to almost 5 liters, was given new cylinder barrels of an extreme 88-millimeter (3.46-inch) bore, while the 68-millimeter (2.68-inch) stroke was retained, giving the engine a displacement of 4,961.576 cubic centimeters (302.7 cubic inches). Utilizing three twin-choke 42DCZ Weber downdraft carburetors and a compression ratio of 8.5:1, the sixty-degree V12 now delivered 340 horsepower at 6,000 revolutions per minute, and versions produced in 1958 and 1959, with 9:1 compression, developed a staggering 400 horsepower at 6,500 revolutions per minute.

Of course, at this point in history Ferrari was planning to sell cars in the United States, where such excessive power was the sine qua non. But for Ferrari, this was to be the largest displacement engine ever to power a touring car.

The chassis of the 410 employed designs already in use on the 250 GT, specifically the front suspension, where the single transverse leaf spring used to support the A-arms on the 375 was replaced by coil springs, as had been done on the Europa GT. Both the front and

rear track were also increased from the 375 model by 130 millimeters, to 1,455 millimeters (58.4 inches) and 1,450 millimeters (58.2 inches), respectively. Chassis length remained at 2,800 millimeters (110.0 inches) until the 1958 and 1959 models, which were reduced to 2,600 millimeters (102.3 inches).

The styling of Pinin Farina's 410 Superamerica was quite similar to a trio of Boano-bodied 250 GTs, also of 1956. This, however, was not unusual, as Pinin Farina and the Boano organization (which

produced the Ferrari 250 GT Boano/Ellena 1956–1958) occasionally collaborated, and at times it was difficult to tell one coachbuilder's car from the other's except for the Farina emblem, or the lack of a body maker's insignia on the Boano-built cars.

For 1956, Ferrari's Gran Turismo cars included the Boano 250 GT coupe, the Scaglietti lightweight 250 GT Berlinetta, at this time produced in very limited numbers almost exclusively for competition-minded customers, and the equally limited-production 410 SA coupe, built in no greater volume than one per month.

Although no two 410 Superamericas were exactly alike, those bodied by Pinin Farina were similar in appearance and considered the most aggressive yet offered as Ferrari road cars. In 1956 the 410 Superamerica sold for an astounding $16,800. To even begin to put that in perspective, the most expensive American car in 1956, the Cadillac Fleetwood Seventy-Five Limousine, sold for $6,240. Even a year later, when Cadillac introduced the ultra-luxury Eldorado Brougham, with the highest price for any American car of its day, it was still more than $3,000 *less* than the Ferrari.

With such a high price, it is no wonder that only fourteen Superamericas were produced: their serial numbers (odd numbers only) were from 0423 SA to 0497 SA. Ghia and Boano also produced coachwork for this model: Ghia built one coupe, the radical Chrysler Gilda and the Dart-inspired 410 Superamerica, while Boano produced a single convertible and coupe. Pinin Farina prepared a luxury,

Opposite: Battista Pinin Farina was also testing the waters with a 1956 concept car, the Superfast I, built on chassis 0483 SA. For this model, the coachbuilder shortened the Superamerica chassis by 20 centimeters. One of the first cars to propose enclosed headlights, the Superfast I also featured a pillarless windshield.

custom-built model, the Superfast I, number 0483 SA. This was a very special model on a shortened 410 SA chassis, which had been fitted with the twin-ignition racing engine used in the Scaglietti-bodied 410 Sport Spyders. Other features of the Grugliasco designer's genius on this car were faired headlights, the large, oval grille, and the pillarless windshield.

In 1956, the short Superfast frame was used for the Series 2 410 Superamerica, of which seven were produced. Two years later, the Series 3 410 Superamerica was introduced in Paris, after having undergone a good number of body-work and engine changes. Approximately twelve examples were produced.

Back in 1952, Ferrari had also decided to continue development of the short-block Colombo-designed V12. Although the larger, long-block Lampredi engine had been successfully converted from a 4.5-liter Grand Prix engine into a suitable sports car power plant, Enzo Ferrari still believed in the original Colombo design.

Since its introduction, the Colombo V12 had been continually improved, increasing the displacement from an initial 1.5 liters to 2.7. In the spring of 1952, another manipulation of the bore and stroke doubled the engine's original swept volume. The new 250 Sport engine, while maintaining the stroke at 58.8 millimeters (2.320 inches), had the bore increased from 70 to 73 millimeters (2.875 inches), for a total displacement of 2,953 cubic centimeters (180 cubic inches). This new engine was fitted with pistons giving a

robust 9.0:1 compression ratio and when paired with three Weber 36 DCF carburetors, it was capable of producing 230 horsepower at 7,500 revolutions per minute.

The revised engine was mounted in a Vignale-bodied Berlinetta similar in appearance to the older 225 Sport, and this was the car Giovanni Bracco drove to victory in the 1952 Mille Miglia.

The Ferrari historian Hans Tanner described the 1952 Italian road race as one of the greatest battles in the history of motor racing, as Bracco took on the whole of the Mercedes-Benz team. Up against bad weather and the incomparable Karl Kling driving a 300 SL, Bracco battled for the lead, gaining and losing it several times until the final leg of the race over the Futa Pass. "Using his knowledge of the treacherous road," wrote Tanner, "Bracco caught up with and passed the Mercedes. When he reached Bologna at the foot of the pass, he was four minutes ahead of Kling, a lead he maintained for the balance of the race through Modena, Reggio, Emilia and Piacenza." This was the only defeat Mercedes-Benz suffered in its championship 1952 season.

The 250 Sport, denoting the new individual cubic centimeter displacement of one cylinder, was used as a test platform in and around Maranello before being handed over to Bracco for the Mille Miglia. The successful debut of the 250 Sport was just the beginning. The car next appeared in the 24 Hours of

The Superfast was also equipped with the twin-ignition racing engine used in the Scaglietti-bodied 410 Sport competition spyders.

Le Mans, this time being driven by Alberto Ascari and Luigi Villoresi. The two led for much of the race but were unfortunately forced to quit after minor mechanical problems put them out. The 250 then appeared at the twelve-hour race at Pescara, once again driven to a first overall by Bracco.

For the final outing of the season, the 250 Sport was taken to the Carrera PanAmericana, where Bracco led for five of the eight legs before having to retire with gearbox failure on the seventh.

Convinced by the success of the 250 Sport, Ferrari decided to put this newly developed engine into a series-built chassis.

However, time was short, and at the 1952 Paris Motor Show only a bare chassis and engine were displayed. Nevertheless, the 250 Sport's legendary season was enough to generate orders for the production version. The original Paris Motor Show chassis was sold in the fall to the Italian movie director Roberto Rossellini and sent to Carrozzeria Vignale for completion as a Competition Spyder.

The production version 250 MM was equipped with twelve port heads and three four-choke 36 IFC/4 Webers. Output was increased from the 250 Sport's 220 horsepower at 7,000 revolutions per minute to 240 horsepower at 7,200 rpm. Both Berlinetta and Spyder configurations were offered with the majority in Berlinetta form bodied by Pinin Farina. A total of twelve Spyders were bodied by Vignale in two distinct series.

At the time, Ferrari had looked upon the 250 Sport merely as a normal evolution of a well-proven and time-tested design. But rather than the last throes of the old Colombo engine, the 250 Sport marked the beginning of Ferrari's longest-running series, the 250 GT. For nearly a decade, some 3,500 motors of almost identical design would power road car and race car alike.

Inside, all of the 410 Superamerica models were lavishly appointed. By the time Series III cars were built, they had reached a new level of fit and finish with the use of supple leather upholstery and leather-covered instrument panels. This car has an offset mounted hand brake (just forward of the driver's seat on the right) but also retains the bracket for mounting the earlier type hand brake under the instrument panel. This was obviously a last minute design change. (*Photographs by Don Spiro*)

This 410 Superamerica has the distinction of carrying the very last Lampredi 4.9-liter V12 built for the series. (*Photographs by Don Spiro*)

250 TR "Testa Rossa"
The Red Head

It was a paint color. To be exact, the red crackle paint used to cover the cylinder heads on the latest derivative of Gioacchino Colombo's V12. Now with a swept volume of 3,000 cubic centimeters, the engine made its debut in November 1957 under the hood of the first customer version of the 250 Testa Rossa, chassis 0710. The silver Ferrari was purchased by the West Coast distributor and race driver John von Neumann, who sent the car from Italy on a circuitous trip to the 1957 Nassau Speed Week event via New York and Florida. The car was driven in Nassau by Richie Ginther, but in its first outing the 250 TR failed to finish. This was to be one of the very few times a 250 TR would not finish a race or, more often, win it. The factory team would win ten of twenty races entered between 1958 and 1961 in World Sports Car Championship events and take the checkered flag at Le Mans in 1958, 1960, and 1961! In addition to the Testa Rossa's three wins at the Circuit de La Sarthe, privately entered 250 Testa Rossas finished fifth and sixth at Le Mans in 1958.

The earliest V12 models featured distinctive coachwork by Scaglietti with bold, pontoon-style cutaway front fenders that left the massive oval grille standing alone. Later versions, like the silver example shown, chassis 0672, also once owned by John von Neumann, had the smoother fender line integrated into the grille. Neither twelve-cylinder model, however, was the first Ferrari to bear the Testa Rossa name.

The first Testa Rossas were powered by a four-cylinder Ferrari engine replete with red crackle paint that had evolved from the factory's earlier 2-liter Mondial race cars. There were Series 1 (1954) and Series 2 Mondials (1955–1957), both with four-cylinder engines. The Mondials, unfortunately, proved no match for the new 2-liter Maseratis. The first Testa Rossas, the Tipo 500 TRC, built in 1956–57, had a swept volume of 2,000 cubic centimeters (versus 1,984.8 cubic centimeters for the Mondial) and 190 horsepower, 30 more than the Series 1 and 20 more than the Series 2 Mondials. These first Testa Rossas won numerous international championship races, including the 2-liter class and second overall at Nassau in 1956, with a repeat in 1957, the 2-liter class in the 1957 Mille Miglia, the 1000km of Buenos Aires and Venezuela; and, in America, the 500 TRCs won top-place standing in class for the 1958 USAC Championship. The 2-liter Testa Rossa was discontinued in 1957, when Ferrari introduced the new 3-liter 250 TR model.

The 250 TR was the ideal vehicle for reviving Colombo's seasoned V12 engine, now at

2,953 cubic centimeters, with a phalanx of six twin-choke Webers and a stirring output of 300 horsepower. Top speed, dependent upon gearing, was more than 170 miles per hour.

The frame for the 250 Testa Rossa was along lines similar to those of the 300 SL and Maserati Birdcage, utilizing a multitube configuration beneath the stunning Scaglietti coachwork. Sergio Scaglietti not only built the 250 TR but designed it as well. The *Gabbia* or cage (thus the Maserati's designation Birdcage) was just that, a complete metal framework matching the contours of the outer skin, which was shaped on styling bucks and attached over the metal substructure. The Testa Rossa is regarded as one of the most visceral sports car designs of all time.

As functional as they were beautiful, the massive long nose and grille were designed to draw as much air as possible to the brakes and radiator. The projecting pontoon fenders housed the covered headlights, giving the car its striking appearance but not offering the aerodynamic advantages of the more enveloped body design introduced with the Series 2 Testa Rossa.

The balance of the 250 TR's underpinnings were Ferrari's "conventional" bill of fare—an independent front suspension utilizing coil springs, live rear axle with semielliptical springs, drum brakes, and a four-speed all-synchromesh gearbox located up front. Nothing was strikingly new about the driveline, only the increased power and the remarkable coachwork, which had been crafted by Carrozzeria Scaglietti. That, however, was enough.

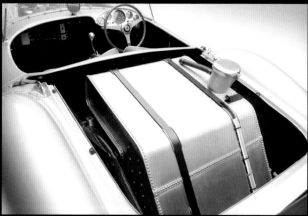

Above and facing page:
Testa Rossa meant "Red Head." To be exact, the red crackle paint used to cover the cylinder heads on the latest derivative of Gioacchino Colombo's V12. The 250 TR was the ideal vehicle for reviving the seasoned V12, now at 2,953 cubic centimeters, with a phalanx of six twin-choke Webers and a stirring output of 300 horsepower. Top speed, dependent upon gearing, was more than 170 miles per hour. Note that the inside of rear deck lid is signed by John von Neumann. The fuel tank for the 250 TR consumed the entire rear of the car with the filler ac-

Coachwork for the Testa Rossa was by Carrozzeria Scaglietti in Modena.

Right: The later Testa Rossa models had their front fenders integrated into the body, giving the cars a more aerodynamic profile, compared with the earlier pontoon fender design.

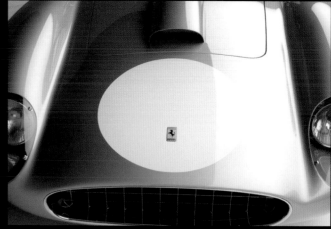

Sergio Scaglietti penned what is arguably the most beautiful sports racing car ever. From any angle the 250 TR is a study in flowing contours that surround one of the most successful engine and driveline combinations of the 1950s.

The silver Series 2 car pictured, serial number 0672, is from the Bruce Meyer collection and began life as one of only two 1957 TRC 625 models. Now considered a TRC 625/250 TR, it was originally purchased by the West Coast Ferrari importer and race driver John von Neumann and campaigned in Southern California by von Neumann and Richie Ginther.

John von Neumann had one of the most important distributorships in the country, Southern California, where he was the importer for both Porsche and Ferrari, about as good as it got in the 1950s and '60s. When Ferrari introduced the 500 TRC, it was von Neumann who convinced Enzo to built two Testa Rossas with the 2.5-liter Le Mans engines, one of which was 0672. (The 625 was a four-cylinder 2.5-liter Grand Prix engine, whereas the 250 TR was the new 3.0-liter V12 evolved from the original Colombo design.) The first of the two 2.5-liter cars, it was shipped to the Auto Club of Mexico on March 24, 1956, where it remained in storage until von Neumann raced it at Avandaro in April. His first time

The driver's head fairing concealed the fuel filler, which was located beneath the cantilevered rear deck lid.

Like all Ferrari race cars, the 250 TR was right-hand drive, with the shifter to the driver's left. The large central tachometer was the most important gauge on the panel, with redline indicated at 6,500 revolutions per minute. Oil temperature, oil pressure, fuel level, and water temperature completed the instrumentation. There was no need for a speedometer. It was part of the pit crew's job to compute speed and lap times.

behind the wheel of the Testa Rossa earned him a checkered flag. The car was then shipped back to Precision Motors in Los Angeles, where Richie Ginther and von Neumann campaigned 0672 for the balance of the 1957 racing season. Including victories at Santa Barbara, Salt Lake City, Pomona, Sacramento, and San Diego, the Testa Rossa and its two seasoned drivers won a total of eleven races by year's end.

The following year, 0672 was refitted with the new 250 Testa Rossa engine. Unfortunately, in 1958, the stars were not aligned for the 250 TR or for Ginther and von Neumann. Ginther won only a single race in Mexico City. Two years later he blew up the engine at the Times-Mirror Grand Prix at Riverside, and in 1961 von Neumann sold 0672 to his fellow auto importer and race team owner Otto Zipper. The Testa Rossa began a new life with Zipper's team under the skilled hands of the legendary Ken Miles. The car's first outing for Otto Zipper's racing team was at Santa Barbara in May 1962, where Miles handily won the event. Later in the year, Miles blew up the engine at Pomona, and Zipper decided to retire the six-year-old race car. By then John von Neumann had retired as well, not only from racing but from his import business, after selling his Southern California region dealership to Volkswagen AG and becoming a very wealthy man.

As for 0672, it has been flawlessly restored and has a very nice home in Bruce Meyer's garage.

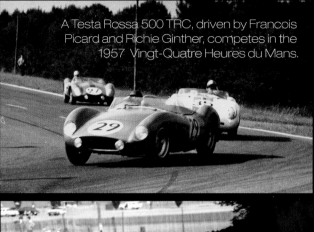

A Testa Rossa 500 TRC, driven by Francois Picard and Richie Ginther, competes in the 1957 Vingt-Quatre Heures du Mans.

Owner John von Neumann raced 0672 at the Pomona L.A. City fair grounds in 1959. (*Photograph by Dave Friedman*)

Driving for the Otto Zipper team in 1960, Ken Miles pilots the number 0672 Testa Rossa at Riverside International Raceway. (*Photograph by Dave Friedman*)

Richie Ginther sits behind the wheel, guiding the 250 TR off the car hauler before the race at Pomona in 1959.

Bottom right: John von Neumann and 0672 at the Santa Barbara races in September 1958. (*Photograph by Dave Friedman*)

Bottom center: Ginther (left) and John von Neumann discuss the 250 TR prior to a race in the late 1950s.

The design for the 250 GT Berlinetta Tour de France followed the Mercedes-Benz 300 SLR accident at Le Mans in 1955. This tragedy marked a turning point for sports car racing, which had progressed to where competition sports cars were closer to Grand Prix cars. As a result, the Fédération Internationale de l'Automobile created new racing classes, and with help from Pinin Farina, Ferrari was ready to compete in the new GT category by 1956 with the 250 GT (Grand Touring) Berlinetta Tour de France.

The Tour de France was a sleek, closed car designed specifically for racing. By design, a Berlinetta is a lightweight, streamlined body trimmed for racing—this being the distinguishing characteristic between a Berlinetta and a traditional coupe. The first series Tour de France, such as this 1956 model owned today by Richard Gent, were unlike any Ferrari competition sports cars.

Below: Enzo Ferrari watches as his mechanics work on a V12 engine in 1953.

Within the Ferrari lineage, the 250 GT SWB Berlinetta was one of those rare cars afforded legendary status by sports car enthusiasts from the day it was introduced. Why this model, designed for Ferrari by the distinguished engineer Giotto Bizzarini (who would later go out on his own and build sports cars)? It was simply the right car at the right moment, introduced on the heels of one great design—the 250 GT Berlinetta Tour de France—and preceding an even greater car—the Ferrari 250 GTO. The 250 GT SWB Berlinetta was the veritable bridge between two of Ferrari's most significant road and race cars of the 1950s and '60s.

The design for the 250 GT Berlinetta Tour de France followed the tragic Mercedes-Benz 300 SLR accident at Le Mans in 1955, where the race driver Pierre Levegh was killed after a failed attempt to avoid hitting a slower car. His streamlined Mercedes careened off the back of Lance Macklin's Austin-Healey after Macklin inadvertently cut him off trying to avoid Mike Hawthorne's Jaguar. Levegh's car slammed

into a retaining wall, where it burst into flames, catapulting burning wreckage into the crowd. More than eighty spectators lost their lives in what was to become the worst accident in the history of Le Mans. It also marked a turning point for sports car racing, which by 1955 had progressed to where competition sports cars were closer to Grand Prix cars than to road cars. As a result, the Fédération Internationale de l'Automobile (FIA) created new racing classes under the title Grand Touring. With help from Pinin Farina, Ferrari was ready to compete in the GT category with a brand-new sports car, the 1956 250 GT (Grand Touring) Berlinetta Tour de France. This was a sleek, closed car designed specifically for racing. As Sergio Pininfarina

Their interiors were generally afforded minimal trim, insulation, and accessories, making them louder and less comfortable but not unbearable. As each car was essentially built to order, some were more luxuriously appointed than others, while a few could best be described as having gutted interiors. This example managed to combine the best of both, and even throw in some fitted luggage.

explained to the author some years ago, a Berlinetta by definition is a lightweight, streamlined body trimmed for racing—this being the distinguishing characteristic between a Berlinetta and a traditional coupe. Berlinetta actually means "little sedan" in Italian. Their interiors were generally afforded minimal trim, insulation, and accessories, making them louder and less comfortable but not unbearable. As each car was essentially built to order, some were more luxuriously appointed than others, while a few could best be described as having gutted interiors.

The Tour de France, a name affectionately given the early 250 GTs following their domination of the ten-day-long race in 1956, remained in production until 1959, by which time the new SWB Berlinetta was waiting in the wings.

Far removed from the competition scene was another Ferrari, also called 250 GT, this a pure road car produced by Pininfarina, which formally changed the spelling of its name to one word in 1958, after the design firm opened new facilities in Grugliasco, outside Turin. The 250 GT PF coupe became the first standard-production Ferrari sports car. Thus, the Gran Turismo initials have been variously applied to any number of Ferraris. The 250 GT SWB Berlinetta, however, was by no means a *typical* road car.

Bizzarini, Carlo Chiti, and Mauro Forghieri had completed development of the prototype in 1959, utilizing a wheelbase measuring only 94.5 inches. The new car used a solid rear axle located in

Under the hood, the Tour de France was all business with the 250 GT engine delivering 240 horsepower at 7,000 revolutions per minute. The V12 breathed through three Weber 36 DCF carburetors.

such a way that an independent rear suspension would have provided no advantage. The front suspension was wishbones and coil springs with an antiroll bar—the rigid axle rear, leaf springs, and radius arms.

Bizzarini's goal had been to improve the handling of the long-wheelbase 250 GT, and this he skillfully accomplished with the SWB Berlinetta. Although the pure road car or Lusso models were

The second series Tour de France was an even more astounding car with bold new styling and distinctive high-crowned front fenders and rear tail fins. The TDF remained in production until 1959. The example shown from the Ron Busuttil collection was built in 1958.

more softly sprung, the hard suspension of the competition version gave the 250 SWB terrific cornering power in exchange for its harsher ride.

Ferrari unveiled the 250 GT SWB Berlinetta at the Paris Motor Show in October 1959. On the short 94.5-inch wheelbase, overall length was only 163.5 inches, (13.6 feet). The blunt-looking fastback carried a classic Colombo-designed sixty-degree, 3.0-liter V12 beneath its elongated hood.

As a result of the GT's redesign, shorter overall length, reduced weight, and increased output—280 horsepower at 7,000 revolutions per minute versus 260 horsepower at 7,000 rpm for the Tour de France—the SWB 250 GT was faster and handled better than its predecessors, making it an even more ominous competitor. All of the cars were equipped with four-speed synchromesh gearboxes, and later models were offered with electric overdrive. The 250 GT SWB Berlinetta was also the first GT Ferrari offered with disc brakes. (Ferrari

A new instrument panel with a black crinkle finish appeared on the second series TDF and a new instrument package provided better positioning of gauges for the driver.

With the hood removed the air box surrounding the Weber 36 DCF carburetors can be seen. This aligned with the hood scoop to force more air into the carburetors.

was late to the game on this feature, following most of his competitors.) The car was the hit of the Paris Motor Show, and order books were soon full, much to the frustration of would-be owners, who were given no delivery date if their names were not known to be directly related to racing!

The Pininfarina design bodies were produced for Ferrari by Scaglietti in Modena. In creating a design to fit the shortened wheelbase, Pininfarina eliminated the use of quarter windows, adding to the car's aggressive and shortened appearance, almost hunched at the back, like a wild cat about to lunge on its prey, which on the racetrack was an apt metaphor for the 250 GT SWB. Most of the bodies were steel, with aluminum doors, hoods, and trunk lids, although a few all-aluminum SWB bodies were built to order for competition. Pininfarina actually manufactured certain components for the steel-bodied cars, while the doors, hoods, and deck lids were all constructed at Scaglietti.

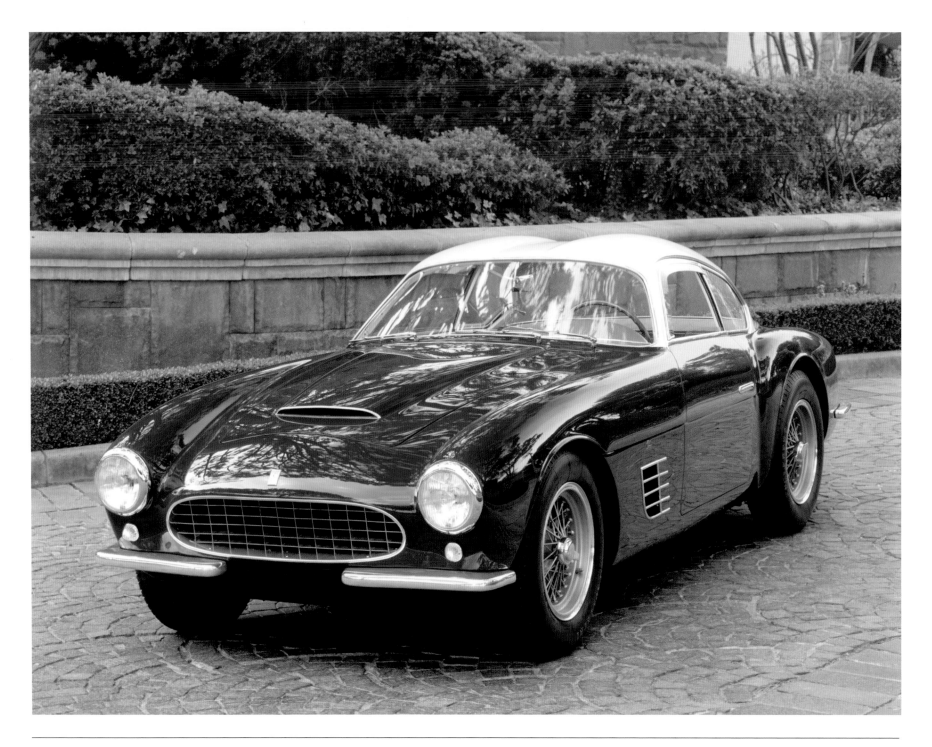

The most distinctive of all Tour de France models was this example designed and bodied by Carrozzeria Zagato. Ugo Zagato's designers penned this "double bubble" Berlinetta in 1956 with a roof line that featured raised sections over the seats, an idea Zagato used more than once in their race car designs to give drivers a little more head room. Seen in the rear three-quarter view is another unique Zagato styling cue, the "Z" configuration of the rear quarter window and backlight pillar. The Carrozzeria's stylists also lent their hand to the interior, not only in the handsome two-tone color combination of the upholstery but in the matching padded dashboard.

Used for both racing and concours by the original owner, the sporty Zagato was powered by the 250 GT engine made popular in more than 2,500 Ferraris built from 1954 to 1964. The car is now part of the David Sydorick collection.

Special racing versions of the 250 GT SWB, with either all-alloy or steel-and-alloy bodies, could be equipped with a larger fuel tank, necessitating relocation of the spare tire directly under the rear window. Additionally, a few 250 GT SWB competition models were built with tuned Testa Rossa engines and six carburetors, thus delivering 300 horsepower.

At the time of its introduction, the 250 GT SWB was a contemporary of the Aston Martin DB 2/4 MK III, Jaguar XK-150 S, Maserati 3500, Mercedes-Benz 300 SL, and Chevrolet Corvette. As a road car, it was without peer, and in competition the 250 GTs quickly ran up a string of victories throughout Europe. In 1960, SWB Berlinettas won the Tourist Trophy race in England, the Tour de France, and the 1000km of Paris at Montlhéry. In 1961, Stirling Moss, driving Rob Walker's SWB, won the Tourist Trophy for Ferrari a second time. In fact, during 1961 so many class wins were collected by SWB Berlinettas, that when the season came to a close, Ferrari owned the GT class in the Constructors' Championship.

The 250 GT SWB Berlinetta was unveiled at the Paris Motor Show in October 1959. On the short 94.5-inch wheelbase, overall length was only 163.5 inches (13.6 feet). The blunt-looking fastback carried a classic Colombo-designed sixty-degree, 3.0-liter V12 beneath its elongated hood.

Left: Giotto Bizzarini, Carlo Chiti, and Mauro Forghieri developed the 250 GT SWB (Short Wheelbase Berlinetta) prototype in 1959, utilizing a wheelbase measuring only 94.5 inches. The new car used a solid rear axle but located in such a way that an independent rear suspension would have provided no additional advantage. The front suspension was wishbones and coil springs with an antiroll bar—the rigid axle rear, leaf springs, and radius arms. The example shown, serial number 2689, is owned today by Bruce Meyer. In 1961 this car won the GT class at Le Mans. It is one of only five ultralightweight factory cars built specifically for the 1961 race.

Every Ferrari dashboard was designed to be functional, but not always attractive. As a purebred race car the SWB's interior fell into the latter category.

Below: With the fuel filler coming through the left rear fender, a splash shield was mounted above the left exhaust pipes, just in case of a fuel spill.

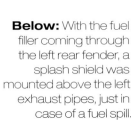

With a top speed around 150 miles per hour, the 250 GT SWB Berlinetta was one of the fastest sports cars of its time, a driver's car with nimble handling and superb balance that allowed it to be driven hard into corners as well as flat out on a straightaway. It was, as one driver wrote, "so easy and comfortable to drive fast, and so sure footed." The 250 GT SWB, in either Lusso or *competizione*, wrote Hans Tanner, "more than any Ferrari before or since, was a car equally at home on a race track or a boulevard." There were fewer than two hundred examples built from late 1959 until early 1963 in both competition and road car versions.

The example pictured from the Bruce Meyer collection is one of the most famous of all the 250 SWB models. Chassis 2689, this factory race car fitted with the ultralightweight body (one of five built for the race at Le Mans) was first in class in 1961, first overall at

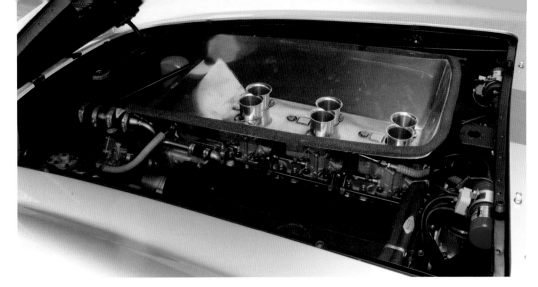

A stirring 260 horsepower lived under the hood of the 250 GT SWB. Swept volume was 2,953.21 cubic centimeters from a bore x stroke of 73 x 58.8 millimeters. Compression ratio was 9.2:1, with the air/fuel mixture dispensed through three Weber 38 DCN carburetors.

Monza in 1961, first in class at the 1961 1000km at Montlhéry, first overall in the 1962 Coupe de Bruxelles, second overall in the 1962 500km at Spa, and second in class at the 1962 Nürburgring 1000km.

These special competition cars were further equipped with higher-output engines utilizing extra-large 46DCF Weber carburetors. Output was boosted to 285 horsepower, and the top speed recorded down the Mulsane Straight at Le Mans was 160 miles per hour.

Throughout Ferrari's early history, the Road from Maranello was paved with legendary cars like the SWB Berlinetta—road cars that could go racing and race cars that could go touring. For the 1950s and early 1960s, owning almost any Ferrari 250 GT model truly was the best of both worlds.

A special poster was made for the 1961 Le Man's winning Ferrari by owner Bruce Meyer. The list of victories by this single car makes it one of the most revered of all 250 GT SWB models. In addition to Le Mans are a first overall at Monza, 1961; first in class 1000km at Montlhéry, 1961; first overall, Coupe de Bruxelles, 1962; second overall, 5000km at Spa, 1962; and second in class at the Nürburgring 1000km, 1962.

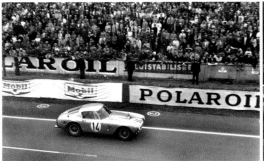

Le Mans 1961 and the 250 GT SWB races on to win its class in the twenty-four-hour day-into-night marathon.

Ferrari 250 GTO
Gran Turismo Omologato

The 250 GTO has accurately been described as beautiful and sinister. Whether at work or at rest, the car radiates a sense of urgency and almost unbridled power. At full throttle, it cuts through the wind as if it were running in a perfect vacuum.

Considered by many to be the most beautiful shape ever to grace an automobile, the Ferrari 250 GTO, the contraction for *Gran Turismo Omologato* (*Omologato* signifying homologated), was the quintessential Ferrari of the 1960s. The majority of GTO bodies were designed by Sergio Scaglietti and built for Ferrari by Carrozzeria Scaglietti in Modena, just a few miles down the road from the Ferrari factory.

Introduced in 1962, the 250 GTO became the preeminent Ferrari road and race car. Only thirty-nine were produced through 1964, making this one of Ferrari's rarest and most valuable models. It would be unusual to see one change hands today for less than $5.5 to 6.0 million.

Essentially a refined version of the 250 GT SWB Berlinetta (1959–62), the 250 GTO was equipped with an improved 3-liter V12 engine carrying six twin-throat Weber 38DCN carburetors, a five-speed, all-synchromesh gearbox (replacing the four-speed used in the 250 GT SWB), and delivering a minimum of 300 horsepower at 8,400 revolutions per minute.

With its engine set deeper in the newly stiffened GTO chassis and pushed back toward the firewall, the engine location lowered the entire car's center of gravity and created an almost perfect weight balance and power distribution. When the car's 300 horsepower was combined with its aerodynamic shape, the result was beyond comprehension. Into, through, and out of the corners, the 250 GTO was poised. And down the straights, it was simply unmatchable and unbeatable. This car is now part of the Chip Connor collection.

One of the principal reasons that Ferrari had developed the GTO was the aerodynamic limitations that 250 GT SWB bodies had encountered at speeds above 155 miles per hour—the blunt front end of the Short Wheelbase Berlinetta hitting the wall, so to speak. The GTO then was a stretched SWB using aerodynamics as a styling guide. The design work at Scaglietti was supervised by Giotto Bizzarini. As an alumnus of the University of Pisa, he was allowed to use the university's wind tunnel, and many of the styling refinements for the GTO came from his work at Pisa. The body design included numerous vents and openings to cool everything from the engine compartment to the brakes while at the same time decreasing the car's coefficient of drag. The net result was an increase in top speed from 155 to 170 mph,

The GTO was the inspiration for a number of sports cars that featured this stylish fastback styling and rear spoiler treatment. The rear fender cutouts were used to vent brake heat.

To make the new car slipperier in the wind, a higher roof line and taller front windshield were installed. These gave the GTO a more aggressive stance than the 250 GT SWB. The rear quarter panels bulged over the deep-set and enlarged rear wheels; the nose of the car was lowered so that the wind would slip invisibly over and around the higher windshield. And the new, lowered front end also helped to eliminate drifting, which sometimes plagued the 250 GT SWB. The GTO's back end was simply cut off behind the rear wheels and crowned with a pronounced ducktail spoiler, which made the car as sleek in the eyes of the wind as any Ferrari GT had ever been. Three half-moon vents cut into the leading edge of the front hood

and ventilation gills sliced behind both the front and rear wheel wells made the car look as much like a shark on the attack as it did a race car on the run.

In order for the car to be homologated for racing, Ferrari was required by the FIA to produce one hundred examples. At the time the cars were to be homologated, in 1962, Enzo Ferrari had produced fewer then one-third of the necessary examples. When pressed by the international racing organization as to whether he intended to build the balance of cars required, Ferrari left the Federation directors stunned by his response: "The market for such a car was already saturated and there were only a few men in the world who could

master its ferocity!" A bombastic way of telling them no, as only Enzo
Ferrari could, and no is no, even in Italian.

Given that the 250 GTO was regarded by the Ferrari factory as merely
an "improved version" of the 250 GT Short Wheelbase Berlinetta, as
modified by Giotto Bizzarini and Sergio Scaglietti in 1961–62, the FIA,
counting all the 250 SWBs that had been built, acquiesced to Ferrari's position and homologated the 250 GTO without further question, opening
the door for one of history's greatest *gran turismos*.

In point of fact, there was some truth to Ferrari's claims, since the GTO
chassis was of the same tubular-type construction as the 250 GT SWB's,
with an independent front suspension and live rear axle. The basic improvements over the Short Wheelbase Berlinetta were dry sump lubrication, a new five-speed gearbox, and a more aerodynamic body. It was a
thinly disguised lie, but no one dared challenge Il Commendatore.

As expected, the cars were virtually unbeatable, and the 250 GTOs
brought Ferrari the coveted Manufacturer's World Championship of
sports cars for three consecutive years—1962, 1963, and 1964 with a total
of twenty first-place finishes in twenty-eight races, fifteen seconds, and
nine thirds!

There are many who consider the Ferrari 250 GTO the most beautiful automobile ever created. While that opinion is open for debate, there
is no question that the 250 GTO is one of the ten greatest cars in automotive history. Its styling is unrivaled by any sports car, past or present.
Its performance, even forty-two years after the last 250 GTO was built, is

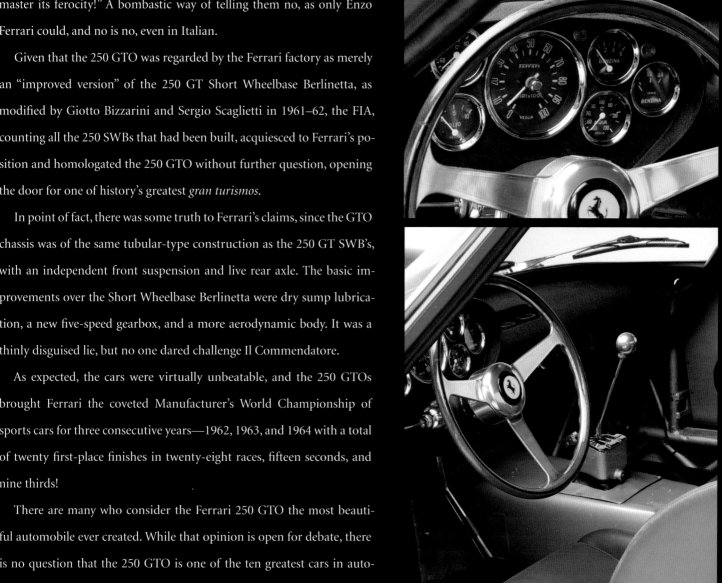

Not a trace of inte-
rior luxury—just pure
race car function in-
side the 250 GTO, yet
despite its austere fur-
nishings, the main in-
strument panel and
steering wheel were
the same as every 250
GT model. The seats
were lightweight rac-
ing seats with leather
upholstery. The rest
of the interior was
painted metal. Note
the emergency brake
positioned alongside
the center tunnel just
right of the foot box.

Car number 24 at the start of the 1963 *Vingt-Quatre Heures du Mans*. (*Photograph courtesy Chip Connor*)

Car 24 on its way to victory circle at Le Mans in 1963. (*Photograph courtesy Chip Connor*)

Next stop victory lane and another chapter in the history of Ferrari at Le Mans. (*Photograph courtesy Chip Connor*)

awe-inspiring. The 250 GTO has become the rarest and most desirable road-race car ever to bear the Cavallino Rampante emblem.

The striking Ferrari red 250 GTO pictured in this chapter, and on the cover of the book, was first in class at Le Mans and second overall in June 1963. It has had what could be called a storybook life: a winner from the start as a factory race car, never crashed, and has gone from one great owner to another for more than four decades. It was restored by none other than the World Driving Champion and former Ferrari *pilota* Phil Hill. This championship Ferrari 250 GTO, chassis no. 4293 GT, is now part of the William E. Connor collection.

500 Mondial
The Four-Cylinder Ferrari

One of the first six 500 Mondial race cars built, this example, bodied by Pinin Farina, was retained by Ferrari for the factory team. A Mondial finished an outstanding second overall in the 1953 Mille Miglia, and the cars were very successful in 1954, winning their classes at Casablanca, Agadir, and Dakar in North Africa. Later, Mike Hawthorne and Umberto Magioli scored a magnificent victory at the Supercortemaggiore Grand Prix at Monza by outrunning the larger three-liter cars!

The twelve-cylinder Ferraris are so revered these days, we often forget the small four-cylinder Mondial models built in the early 1950s. The 500 Mondial was simply the sports car version of the highly successful 2.0-liter single-seat race cars that won the championship for Ferrari (driven by Ascari) in 1952 and 1953. The Mondial's Lampredi-designed racing engine featured twin overhead camshafts, dual magneto ignition, dry sump lubrication, roller tappet cam followers, and two Weber 40 DCO A3 carburetors working in concert to deliver a conservative 160 horsepower at 7,000 revolutions per minute to the rear wheels.

The power was delivered via a multiplate clutch and four-speed transaxle mounted at the rear of the chassis. Also, as in the single-seat

The 500 Mondial was a sports car version of the highly successful 2.0-liter single-seat race cars. The Mondial's Lampredi-designed racing engine featured twin overhead camshafts, dual magneto ignition, dry sump lubrication, roller tappet cam followers, and two Weber 40 DCO A3 carburetors working in concert to deliver a conservative 160 horsepower at 7,000 revolutions per minute to the rear wheels.

2.0-liter race cars, the front suspension was independent by unequal length A-arms. The rear suspension was a de Dion axle supported by a transverse leaf spring.

The car pictured, serial number 0418, is one of the first six built that were retained by Ferrari for the factory team. The first half of the total of thirty-four cars built were bodied by Pinin Farina and the remainder by Carrozzeria Scaglietti.

A Mondial finished an outstanding second overall in the 1953 Mille Miglia, and the cars were very successful in 1954, winning their classes at Casablanca, Agadir, and Dakar in North Africa. Later, Mike Hawthorne and Umberto Magioli scored a magnificent victory at the Supercortemaggiore Grand Prix at Monza by outrunning the larger three-liter cars!

The 500 Mondial continued to be successful throughout the early 1950s in the hands of privateer race drivers, making them one of the most coveted, but least popularized of early Ferrari models.

*"I never thought a son could leave his father a legacy but my son did;
for it was only after he had passed away that I realized to the full
the goodness of this young man, who knew he was going to die
yet never inflicted the burden of his infinite suffering either
on me, his father, or on the friends who went to see him."*

—*Enzo Ferrari*

The Ferrari legend would not be complete without the Dino, even though it is a Fiat, not a Ferrari. In a very lose interpretation, the Dino is to Ferrari what the 914 was to Porsche, a less expensive companion model built by another company. (In Europe the 914 was a Volkswagen, not a Porsche.)

For Enzo Ferrari, the reasons for producing the Dino were not based on economies of scale; they were very personal and, in fact, led to his decision to write his memoirs in 1963. "The death of my son Dino," wrote Ferrari, "induced me to pause sadly and reflect. Catching my breath, I looked back down the long road I have traveled. With my life stretched away behind me, I decided to find release in this dialogue with myself, hoping it would not be too late; a dialogue in solitude, in the shadow of the greatest sorrow of my life."

The V6 Dino models were produced to commemorate Il Commendatore's son, who had died in 1956.

"He was born into motor racing," wrote Enzo. "He became a motor racing enthusiast to the exclusion of all other sports and himself drove with skill the various cars I let him have. The first was a little Fiat Toplino 500; after this came a Fiat 100TV and, finally, a 2-liter Ferrari that he would now and again take to

The Dino design by Pininfarina was one of the most curvaceous bodies ever produced for a sports car, a fact that contributed to the Dino's longevity. The 206GTs were the only Dinos bodied in aluminum. Designed by Pininfarina, the coachwork was built by Scaglietti while the alloy engines were produced by Fiat. Dino production started early in 1969. The cars bore no Ferrari emblems, and the only reference to Ferrari was the Dino GT name next to the taillights and the Pininfarina body plate forward of the rear wheel well. The cars were produced on a 2,336-millimeter (92.1-inch) wheelbase welded tubular steel frame with four-wheel independent suspension and disc brakes.

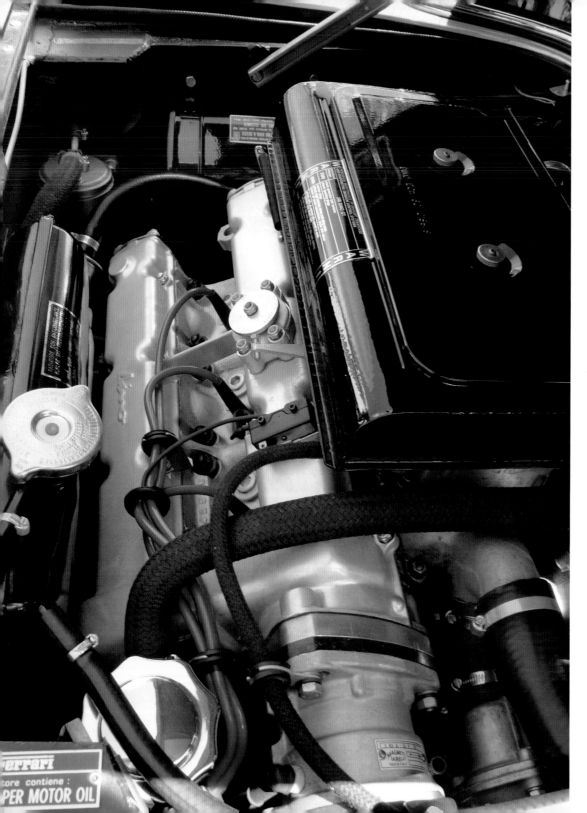

the Modena track to try out. This passion of his was a cause of concern to me, not so much for any risks he might run, but because his health was precarious and I was afraid he might overtax himself."

Although Alfredo "Dino" Ferrari had suffered from muscular dystrophy since birth, he had his father's indomitable will. He managed to get through school and acquire a degree in engineering, but as his health began to fail in his early twenties, Dino was forced to spend most of his time in bed. Enzo and his close friend the brilliant engineer Vittorio Jano, whom Ferrari had hired away from Fiat back in the 1920s, would spend time with him discussing Dino's designs for a new 1.5-liter racing engine. Dino had even written a two-part article on the design of his high-performance V6 engine in the Italian magazine *Velocita*. "For reasons of mechanical efficiency," noted Enzo, "[Dino] had finally come to the conclusion that the engine should be a V6 and we accepted his decision." Five months after Dino passed away, Ferrari built his son's engine, the 156 Dino.

"He was a young man with a surprisingly serene outlook. When I was worried about something, for instance, he never failed to have a soothing word for me. He was young, but he always had the right word ready at the right moment," wrote

The engine in the first Dino model, the 206GT, was a 180-horsepower, sixty-five-degree V6 displacing 1,987 cubic centimeters with a bore x stroke of 86 x 57 millimeters. The engines used in the 246GT (pictured) and GTS displaced 2,418 cubic centimeters with a 92.5 x 60 millimeter bore x stroke and increased output to 195 horsepower at 7,600 revolutions per minute.

Enzo. Though his death was an inevitability, when Dino finally succumbed to his illness, it came as a staggering, almost life-altering blow to his father, and, in order to honor Dino's memory, Ferrari developed not only the 156 but an entire line of Dino engines over a ten-year period for use in Formula One, Formula Two, sports racing, and GT road cars.

"I never thought a son could leave his father a legacy," said Enzo, "but my son did; for it was only after he had passed away that I realized to the full the goodness of this young man, who knew he was going to die yet never inflicted the burden of his infinite suffering either on me, his father, or on the friends who went to see him. He was a noble lad and a generous one, and not only because he paid for books and subscriptions to technical journals for his needy friends. Leaving me his great spiritual inheritance, my son above all taught me that we remain children up to all ages, until, tried by some great sorrow, we suddenly learn the meaning of goodness, renunciation, charity and duty. And, too, what life means to a young man who is leaving it."

Knockoff wheels were standard on the Dino 246GT.

In 1965, Carrozzeria Pininfarina bodied the first Dino road car to be powered by the mid-mounted V6 engine. The prototype, known as the Dino 206GT *Speciale*, was displayed at the Paris Motor Show in October. A second version, called the Dino Berlinetta GT, was displayed at the 1966 Turin Motor Show; like that of the earlier example, its engine was positioned longitudinally ahead of the rear axle. A third and final version made its debut at Turin in November 1967; this one had the Fiat-produced engine mounted transversely and built in unit with a five-speed transaxle. An additional prototype was shown in Brussels the following year, and, early in 1969, Dino production started at Carrozzeria Scaglietti. By the end of the year, roughly 150 had been built, all with hand-formed aluminum bodies of exceptional style.

With the engines built by Fiat, the cars had the distinction of being the first production Ferraris to be given only even chassis numbers (road cars had, with few exceptions, been serialized in odd numbers only) and the first to wear neither the Cavallino Rampante

The 246GT Dino succeeded the 206GT at the end of 1969 and remained in production through 1973.

The Dino name was proudly displayed on the hood where a Ferrari emblem would have otherwise been mounted. Owners often replaced the Dino badge with the Cavillino Rampante emblem. Neither the Ferrari nor Fiat name was used on the cars.

The rear styling of the Dino was again the inspiration for numerous sports cars built in the 1970s. The long sail panels and curved-in backlight were benchmark designs.

Far left:
The styling of the Dino by Pininfarina was the inspiration for a number of later sports car designs, but none had the unique character of the Scaglietti-bodied Fiats.

emblem nor the Ferrari name. They simply bore the signature "Dino GT" on the right corner of the body below the engine cover.

The mechanical basis for the 206GT *Speciale* was the 206 engine, which had been built in small numbers for the 1966 racing season. The compact V6 utilized four overhead camshafts, a design descended from the engine of the 1961 1,500-cubic-centimeter Formula One World Championship car. The Dino name was first applied to the engine used in a single-seat Formula Two car, after which

all of the V6 engines, whether for racing or for road cars, were so designated. The 206 identification was derived from the engine's total displacement in deciliters, 206, indicating 20 deciliters or 2 liters, and six cylinders.

In order for Ferrari to use the Dino engine in Formula Two competition, it had to come from a mass-produced automobile of no fewer than five hundred units; thus, Maranello entered into an agreement with Fiat to build five hundred engines and use them in a vehicle that

could quickly attain homologation requirements. This was a hasty but efficient means to an end for Ferrari.

While it is regarded as a Fiat engine, all of the lower part of the Dino—oil sump, gearbox, drive shaft, and differential for each engine—was produced in Maranello by Ferrari and shipped to Fiat for the final assembly, so the engines are as much Ferrari as they are Fiat! The Dino V6 was later found in various forms, in the Fiat Dino Pininfarina Cabriolet, the Fiat Dino Bertone Coupes, the Formula Two sin-gle-seaters, and, of course, in the Dino 206GT, 246GT, and 246GTS. Of the 206GT versions, it is estimated that no more than one hundred were completed before the 246GT took their place. Nearly identical in appearance, the new number designation indicated that the 246GT had a larger swept volume, of 2.4 liters. This was achieved through a new bore x stroke of 92.5 x 60 millimeters. Output was consequently increased from the 206's 180 horsepower at 8,000 revolutions per minute to 195 at 7,600 rpm, and torque was improved to

The Dino 246GTS was added in 1972 and featured a removable Targa-type roof panel. The last Dino model concluded production in 1974. Total numbers for the 206GT, 246GT, and 246GTS far exceeded the original five hundred units Ferrari had been required to build. By the time the Dino was retired from production, more than four thousand had been built, of which twelve hundred were the popular 1972–1974 GTS models.

166 pounds/feet at 5,500 rpm, delivered to the rear wheels via a five-speed, fully synchronized gearbox. Another change was in the wheelbase. The 206 had measured 89.7 inches, whereas the 246GT returned to the earlier Dino prototype's span of 92.1 inches, an increase of 6 centimeters.

With the engine mounted transversely ahead of the rear wheels, the Dino had given the stylists at Pininfarina a fresh canvas upon which to design the body, leading to one of the car's most distinctive features. Aside from being the first Ferrari Gran Turismo with a mid-mounted engine, the Dino featured a concave, vertical backlight wrapping around the front of the engine compartment. This allowed the sides of the roof line to slope into dramatic, flowing sail panels that extended beyond the crown of the rear fenders, thus silhouetting them against the elongated roof line. The aluminum bodies were built at Scaglietti in Modena, giving the Dino yet another significant tie to Maranello. If the Dino's dramatic styling wasn't enough to attract customers, its price certainly was. In 1970, one could purchase a Fiat Dino for just $13,400.

As an automaker, Fiat is one of Italy's oldest and largest, and though not highly regarded in the United States, in Italy, Fiat is the equivalent of General Motors. It is the country's largest automaker and today includes Alfa Romeo, Lancia, and Ferrari among its various holdings. Through the Turin automaker's 105-year history, it had occasionally flirted with greatness, and one of the high-water marks was certainly its collaboration with Enzo Ferrari on the Dino.

The majority of first-series Dinos were sold in Italy and Europe, although a few were brought into the United States by Luigi Chinetti in 1969. The 206GT was replaced at the end of 1969 by the 246GT, which remained in production through 1973. The 246GTS, featuring a removable Targa-type roof panel, was added in 1972 and

concluded Dino production in 1974. Total numbers for the 206GT, 246GT, and 246GTS far exceeded the original five hundred units Ferrari had been required to build. By the time the Dino was retired from production, more than four thousand had been built, of which twelve hundred were the popular 1972–74 GTS models.

Far more than a footnote to Dino history is the Dino-derived V8 engine used in the 1973 Dino 308 GT4 2+2. This brief series of models, with coachwork designed by Bertone, was entirely different in design from the original Dino. One example of the 2+2 was even entered at Le Mans in 1974 by Luigi Chinetti's NART racing team. Yet another version of the Dino, the 2-liter 208 GT4, was sold exclusively in Europe. The end result of the 308 GT4 was the new Ferrari 308 GT, which finally took the place of the Dino in 1975.

Chapter 6

Coming of Age in America—Ferraris of the 1960s and 1970s

In the 1960s and '70s, a generation of Americans was growing up with contempt for authority, government, and possessions. Little did they know of Ferraris, winding mountain roads, and the sound of a V12 echoing in the air.

In the early 1960s, Ferrari introduced one spectacular road car after another. In the wake of the 410 Superamerica came the 250 GTB Lusso, Spyder California, and 500 Superfast, models that would leave enthusiasts muttering to themselves and glorify forever the history of the sports car. The pages of *Road & Track, Sports Car Graphic*, and *Motor Trend*, among others, were continually paying homage to Ferrari with reviews that left enthusiast readers yearning for one of the maker's cars in their garages. Few, however, had the means to fulfill that dream. By the 1960s, a Ferrari was one of the most expensive automobiles in the world and, in some instances, one of the most luxurious.

Luxury is not a word one would immediately associate with Ferrari sports cars of the 1950s, but by the 1960s Enzo Ferrari had come to realize his cars would have to meet the needs and demands of a much diversified clientele. In 1964 *luxury* became a word that one

The stylish 250 GT Cabriolet Series I, introduced in 1957, was a dramatic departure from traditional sports car styling of the period. The design, by Pininfarina, featured an aggressive front-end appearance, accented by headlights faired into the fender line and covered by Perspex, as had been done on 250 GT race cars, an air intake consuming nearly a third of the hood area, and bold chromed vertical bumperettes, flanking the grille and faired into the shape of the fenders.

The 250 GT Cabriolet interior was plush for a Ferrari, with leather-upholstered seating, console, door and kick panels, and a dashboard finished in a glare-resistant, matte black crinkle texture.

could indeed attribute to a Ferrari. That was the year Ferrari introduced the 500 Superfast.

It had been briefly preceded by the 400 Superamerica, a sports car afforded an extra measure of interior luxury and comfort, and thus distinguished from more traditional race-bred road cars. The luxury *Gran Turismo* premise had its beginnings with the 410 Superamerica, but refining the ride and interior, and combining the very best attri-

butes of a road car and a race car in one did not reach maturity until the Superfast was unveiled.

Aside from pure race cars, every Ferrari road car of the 1950s was luxurious for its time. There was, however, what many customers perceived to be a compromise in Maranello's road-going Spyders and Berlinettas, which were tied more closely to the company's racing heritage than to the luxury and comfort one found, for example,

in early postwar Alfa Romeo road cars. This was a point Luigi Chinetti continually brought to Enzo's attention, a bone of contention that seemed to have both men at odds throughout the 1960s.

By the latter half of the 1950s, a persistent demand was arising for a car with more luggage space and more luxurious appointments than Maranello's purebreds had to offer. Bespoke coachwork from Italy's leading ateliers had from time to time risen to the occasion with exquisite two- and four-place creations, but in general a Ferrari was not a luxury car.

The move to lusso styling, luxurious in an American context as Ferrari saw it, didn't happen until the Pininfarina 250 GT 2+2 arrived in 1961. By the end of 1963, more than 950 had been delivered. For Ferrari, such sales for a single model were phenomenal. For Enzo Ferrari, it was almost an epiphany.

The engine in the 250 GT Cabriolet Series I was a Colombo-designed sixty-degree V12 with a bore x stroke of 73 x 58.8 millimeters (2.870 x 2.315 inches) displacing 2,953 cubic centimeters (180 cubic inches). The valve operation was by a single overhead camshaft on each bank with roller followers and rocker arms to inclined valves. With three twin-choke Weber carburetors and a compression ratio of 8.5:1, output from this engine was 240 horsepower at 7,000 revolutions per minute.

The 250 GT Pininfarina Cabriolet was also the star of the 1958 Ferrari exhibit in Paris.

Back in 1957, Ferrari had commenced series production of its first convertible, the 250 GT Cabriolet. The first example designed by Pininfarina was shown at the 1957 Geneva Motor Show. The GT Cabriolet was not intended for competition, although with a 240-horsepower Colombo V12 under the hood, there wasn't much aside from suspension, tuning, and a very plush interior that separated the car from those built for competition. It was perhaps the ideal compromise between the two extremes for the late 1950s.

The Cabriolet's chassis was identical to that of the Boano coupes being produced at the same time, both using a welded oval tubular steel, ladder-type frame with independent front and live rear axle, and drum brakes.

With a handsome if not a stunning design, the early cars were noted for their very dramatic grilles, protruding Perspex-covered headlamps faired into the fender lines, and bold vertical front bumperettes. The Pininfarina design

Far left:
At the 1958 Geneva Motor Show, Ferrari displayed three very different types of sports cars with the Pininfarina Cabriolet stage center.

The 400 Superamerica was afforded an extra measure of interior luxury and comfort, and thus distinguished from more traditional race-bred road cars. The luxury *Gran Turismo* premise had its beginnings with the 410 Superamerica, but refining the ride and interior, and combining the very best attributes of a road car and a race car in one did not entirely succeed with the short-lived 400 Superamerica line.

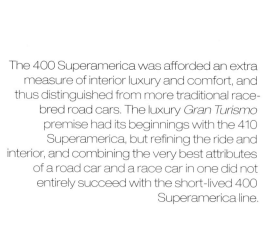

featured a prominent air intake laid almost flat and extending nearly three-quarters of the hood's length. This, along with the headlight and bumper design, gave the car an extremely aggressive appearance from the front. The first-series cars were limited to approximately two dozen examples, all of similar design, while later versions (another twelve cars produced in 1958–59) featured a one-piece, wraparound front bumper and less dramatic uncovered headlights pushed farther out to the corners, giving the front end more of a squared-off appearance. It is estimated that Series I production ran to around forty examples, all with steel bodies by Pininfarina.

While the 250 GT Cabriolet was an excellent compromise between race car and road car, with the emphasis on the latter, in New York, Luigi Chinetti was looking for a more aggressively styled GT convertible to sell. Chinetti's was not the only voice beckoning Enzo to send Pininfarina back to the drawing board and his engineers to task on a revised chassis and suspension. Ferrari's West Coast distributor, the race driver John von Neumann, agreed that the 250 GT Cabriolet was not the kind of Ferrari his customers wanted. He told Enzo that an open car with the characteristics of the lighter Berlinettas would be very popular in the United States. Il Commendatore

In the midst of building road cars, Ferrari also managed to produced two remarkable race cars in the early 1960s, the first being the 250 GT Short Wheelbase Berlinetta.

complied and gave approval for a special series to be built; the 250 GT Spyder California went into limited production in May 1958 and was built through 1960 on the long wheelbase GT Berlinetta chassis.

The revised coachwork, penned by Pininfarina, was once again manufactured at Modena in the workshops of Scaglietti. The cars were produced in two series, the long wheelbase, of which fewer than fifty were built, and the short wheelbase, a lighter weight, steel-and-aluminum-bodied version, introduced in 1960 and built through 1963. The total was again around fifty examples.

According to Enzo Ferrari, the 250 GTO was regarded by the factory as merely an "improved version" of the 250 GT Short Wheelbase Berlinetta, as modified by Giotto Bizzarini and Sergio Scaglietti in 1961-62. This was his rationale for not building the requisite number of 250 GTOs for homologation. The GTO was equipped with an improved 3-liter V12 engine carrying six twin-throat Weber 38DCN carburetors, a five-speed, all-synchromesh gearbox (replacing the four-speed used in the 250 GT SWB), and delivering a minimum of 300 horsepower at 8,400 revolutions per minute.

Regarded as an even sportier version of the Spyder California, the short wheelbase model was built on the same chassis as the 250 GT SWB Berlinetta, measuring 20 centimeters (7.9 inches) less in wheelbase than the first series Spyder California. The SWB cars had essentially the same handling characteristics as the competition-bred Berlinettas and, like the first-series Spyders, were genuine sports cars.

Among a handful that were pressed into competition was one entered by Luigi Chinetti's North American Racing Team and driven by Bob Grossman and Ferdinand Tavano to a fifth overall finish in the 1959 Vingt-Quatre Heures du Mans. Several California Spyders were also fitted with competition engines and, upon special order, supplied with all-aluminum bodies. The cars were otherwise made of steel, with aluminum doors and deck lids.

Luigi Chinetti was looking for a more aggressively styled GT convertible to sell in the late 1950s and early 1960s, as was Ferrari's West Coast distributor John von Neumann. They both agreed that the 250 GT Cabriolet was not the kind of Ferrari their customers wanted. In 1958 Enzo Ferrari took their advice and gave approval for a special series to be built, the 250 GT Spyder California. The first series went into limited production in May 1958 and was built through 1960 on the long wheelbase GT Berlinetta chassis. The car pictured is a 1960 SWB model.

Among the most notable successes for a competition Spyder California was the ninth place overall and GT class win of Richie Ginther and Howard Hively in the 12 Hours of Sebring. Another 250 GT Spyder California, this one driven by Giorgio Scarlatti and Carlo Abate, captured the GT class at the 12 Hours of Sebring in 1960.

The LWB Spyder California was produced in three series. About seven cars were built before the new LWB 250 GT Berlinetta engine and chassis were utilized. It is estimated that twenty-seven second-series cars were produced between the end of 1958 and the end of 1959. Most of the competition versions came out of this production run. The third-series cars were fitted with the outside plug V12 engine, developed from the 250 Testa Rossa, and equipped for the first time with disc brakes. Minor styling changes by Pininfarina to update the cars included reshaping of the rear fenders to reduce their width, a new rear deck, and new one-piece taillights.

Air vents were a styling trait of the Spyder California, although some examples were built without them.

Opposite: The track was widened on SWB models, which were also the first to switch from lever-type shock absorbers to adjustable telescopic units.

The SWB Spyder California made its debut at the Geneva Motor Show in March 1960. These examples were equipped with new heads and larger valves, increasing output by 20 horsepower to 280 horsepower at 7,000 revolutions per minute. (Competition engines were further increased to 300 horsepower with even larger valves, high-lift camshafts, and lighter-weight connecting rods and pistons.) The track was widened on SWB models, which were also the first to switch from lever-type shock absorbers to adjustable telescopic units.

The Spyder California, in either wheelbase, was one of the first Ferraris to be described as a "driver's car," a car that was capable of exceptional speed and handling yet comfortable and luxurious enough for daily driving. The last example (4167 GT) was sold in the United States in February 1963.

At the same time Scaglietti was turning out Spyder Californias, Ferrari took steps to further differentiate the Cabriolet model, introducing the Series II in 1959. This model was built concurrently with

the Spyder California through 1962. Still on the long wheelbase, the Series II Cabriolet was even more of a *boulevardier* than the Series I, with styling similar to the Pininfarina coupe, sans roof. It proved to be one of the most luxurious open Ferraris of the era.

"In Italy, it was hard for the factory to understand a convertible as a serious fast car," explains Luigi Chinetti, Jr. "To them high speed was the domain of the closed car, the Berlinetta, a lightweight, streamlined body trimmed for racing."

Enzo saw things differently, perhaps from a purely Italian perspective. "The sportsman usually goes for the Gran Turismo coupé," he explained. "In most cases he is a gentleman who possesses a good private income, drives passably well and is convinced he knows how to handle a car 'almost like a racing driver.' Some of these customers actually do take part in competitions with their cars and may continue to take an interest in motor sport for quite a number of years if they do not give it up after the first event or two. The man who does go on, however, ends up by becoming an *habitué* of Maranello."

Next Ferrari explained the role of older owners, men he classified as the "fifty-year-olds." This class of customer, he said, "is a large one, a market survey having revealed that 80 percent of Ferrari owners are men with more than half a century behind them. These

The Spyder California's dashboard configuration and finish were virtually identical to the earlier Pininfarina Cabriolet Series I cars. The Spyder California was not as luxuriously upholstered as the Cabriolet, and it had more purposeful interior trim. Some were delivered as special orders with more luxurious interiors, while others were provided minimal trim for competition. The cars used a four-speed all-synchromesh transmission with direct drive in fourth.

By the 1960s the assembly lines in Maranello were humming along at a rate that, by Ferrari's standards, could have been described as "mass production."

The SWB Spyder California made its debut at the Geneva Motor Show in March 1960. These examples were equipped with new heads and larger valves, increasing output by 20 horsepower to 280 horsepower at 7,000 revolutions per minute. (Competition engines were further increased to 300 horsepower with even larger valves, high-lift camshafts, and lighter-weight connecting rods and pistons.)

fifty-year-olds are men who, by making an old dream come true, wish on the one hand to award themselves a sort of prize for the financial position they have managed to build up for themselves and, on the other, to snatch back a little of their youth." Ferrari reasoned that by the end of a week's hard work, these individuals "settle behind the wheel of one of my powerful responsive cars and, in the physical joy of dominating it, find a mental relaxation that takes years off their shoulders." It should be added, he wrote, "that

these cars, with their powerful acceleration, give the driver a strong feeling of security, especially when he has to overtake. We all know, in fact, that on today's crowded roads one must overtake quickly if one is to overtake safely or at all; and the Ferrari, with its rocket-like acceleration, is one of the few cars that allows one to get past in an instant and, thus without risk."

Finally, Ferrari addressed those patrons who had little interest in either racing his cars or Ferrari's history: "a customer who

Chassis number 1803 is the very first 250 GT SWB Spyder California produced. Chassis specifications for the SWB were almost identical to those of the SWB Berlinetta. With a wheelbase of only 94.5 inches and lighter overall weight than the LWB Spyder California, the 1960–63 models were the best handling of the series and the most attractively styled.

has no inkling of how a car works and buys a Ferrari merely because it is, as it were, the mink or—in the case of the Superamerica model—the chinchilla among automobiles. There are not really a great many customers of this kind—far fewer, indeed, than is generally believed. Here at Maranello, we see just a small number of these customers during the course of a year, nearly always accompanied by breathtaking women who exercise a magnetic effect on every mechanic in the workshop. With these clients, the discussion of their car—needing much patience—is chiefly concerned with the color of the body, the shade of the upholstery and the various internal fittings." Ferrari commented that the men taking such orders were sometimes placed in a "most embarrassing—albeit not

always un-amusing—position that does not arise even in the case of professional drivers whose cars are their bread and butter."

In America, the situation was almost the opposite, and the latter two categories of Ferrari owners were the majority, with sportsmen being the foundation of Chinetti's and von Neumann's customers but not the lifeblood. In New York, Chinetti Sr.'s customers were clamoring for an aggressively styled convertible, and the same was true on the West Coast.

"It was with great reluctance that Mr. Ferrari acquiesced to building these cars for the American market," says Luigi Chinetti, Jr. "Ironically," he adds, with an unrestrained smile, "the 250 GT Spyder California turned out to be the most successful Ferrari model sold in this country up to that time!"

*There was one thing that separated Ferrari from
every other imported sports car sold in America...Luigi Chinetti.*

The North American Racing Team (NART) story begins in 1956, just as Ferrari was gaining a solid foothold on American shores. By the early 1960s, NART was blazing across road courses from the East to the West Coast of America. The most important role NART was to play, however, was in its influence on Enzo Ferrari.

At the time, the 250 GT Berlinetta Lusso was the most daring new design from Ferrari and Carrozzeria Pininfarina since the 410 Superamerica. With styling that resembled a touring version of the 250 GTO, the 250 GT Berlinetta Lusso is deemed by many the most beautiful Ferrari ever built. But such acclaim has been conferred upon many Ferraris designed in the 1950s and 1960s, including the 250 GTO.

With the Lusso, Sergio Pininfarina and his staff had delivered the first contemporary Ferrari road car of the new decade. The Lusso body was a series of graceful curves, from the front fenders to the upturned rear spoiler, and free from any superfluous chrome trim to embellish its shape. Antoine Prunet described the new design as Pininfarina's escape from the "cubist" period, which had prevailed through most of the 250 GT and 410 SA models. However, the Lusso actually capitalized on many of those earlier designs. The forward-projected headlamps integrated in the fenders were straight off the Series I Pininfarina Cabriolet. Even the bumper design drew its shape from the bumperettes of the early Cabriolet. Where the Lusso departed from

The 275 GTS/4 NART Spyder was the creation of Luigi Chinetti and Sergio Scaglietti. Based on the 275 GTB/4, the cars were bodied by Scaglietti for exclusive sale in the United States.

past designs was in the rear fender treatment, which began at the windshield pillars and carried all the way back through the tops of the doors until they met with the edge of an abbreviated deck lid—the only flat surface in the entire design. The styling of the Lusso, noted Prunet, "was all in accord with the aerodynamic theories of Doctor Professor Wunibald Kamm of the Stuttgart Technical University, and proven by Pininfarina and Ferrari on the 250 GTO."

Sergio Pininfarina recalls that before the firm had a wind tunnel to test aerodynamics, he used to attach ribbons of wool to the cars and then drive them on the autostrada at high speed to see how they reacted. It was a primitive but effective means of checking the aerodynamic efficiency of a new design—the poor man's version of smoke in a wind tunnel. "That might sound like fun, because everybody likes to drive fast, but when you have to do it, that's different," said Pininfarina. "It took us

The styling of the Lusso inspired a number of subsequent designs, particularly the rear aspect, which appeared again on the new 275 GTB. One of the most interesting characteristics is the narrow rear pillar, giving the car an almost wraparound window effect and virtually no blind spot.

seven years to design, make, test, and start operation of a wind tunnel, which we opened in 1972." Back in the days of the Lusso, however, it was fast driving on the autostrada and lots of wool.

The Lusso's sleek, contoured shape, which pioneered the aerodynamic vogue of the 1960s, was complemented by an interior that was the most luxurious yet for a Ferrari. Within the roomy cabin, driver and passenger sat in true bucket-type seats, upholstered in buttery, hand-sewn Italian leather. The speedometer and tachom-

eter were housed in two large pods, uncharacteristically located in the center of the dashboard, with the smaller secondary gauges set into the dash behind the steering wheel. This unusual instrumentation design was unique to the Lusso. There was also a full luggage shelf behind the seats, as well as a modest trunk, making this the first Ferrari road car that could carry enough luggage to actually take on the road. As such, the Lusso was the kind of car Chinetti was able to sell to his American clientele, who wanted the cachet of

Above: In profile, the Lusso displayed its stunning fender lines, flowing from the headlights through to the truncated rear-deck lid. The styling of the Lusso pioneered the aerodynamic vogue of the 1960s and gave the already long-lived 250 GT chassis a new lease on life. During its two-year production run, approximately 350 were built.

The Lusso interior was unique to this model, with a distinctive, if not unusual, placement of the primary gauges in the center of the dashboard, perhaps to give the passenger an opportunity to note exactly how fast the car was going! For its time, the Lusso interior was exceedingly plush for a Ferrari, with a great deal of attention paid to leather trim and carpeting. The dashboard was also upholstered in non-reflective black leather, lending both a luxurious and a functional touch to the instrument panel.

Within the production run of 275 GTB and 275 GTB/4 models, there were short-nose and long-nose versions, a slightly larger rear window, and exposed trunk hinges. The car pictured is the actual 1966 prototype for the GTB/4 built by Pininfarina and displayed by Ferrari at the 1966 Paris Motor Show. This example exhibits many of the aforementioned traits, including the exposed trunk hinges. The 275 GTB chassis, with a wheelbase of just 94.5 inches, was a proven design of ladder-type welded tubes, with a four-wheel independent suspension consisting of unequal-length A-arms, coil springs, and telescopic shock absorbers.

The door opened just wide enough to settle yourself on the seat and turn into position behind the wheel. This was Maranello's finest example of touring luxury since the days of the 212 Vignale Inter and Export models. Leather was used liberally throughout, from the dashboard and door panels to the adjustable sport seats, center console, and transmission tunnel. The smell was nearly intoxicating, the appearance, aesthetically pleasing to a fault. Sports cars of this ilk were never quite so lavish.

Ferrari ownership with none of the compromises in comfort that came with most models based on Maranello's 250 GT race cars. Aside from exemplary styling and interior design, the 250 GT Berlinetta Lusso was the fastest sports car of its day, with a top speed of 150 miles per hour at 7,400 revolutions per minute.

When the last Lusso pulled away from Maranello at the end of 1964, it marked the beginning of a new era for Ferrari. The 250 GT was gone, but in its place arose a new GT engine, the 275 GT. It was this car, the 275 GTB, which would lead to a quarrel between Enzo Ferrari and Luigi Chinetti, Sr., that they never quite got over.

Introduced as a two-cam model in 1964, the 275 GTB was the first of Ferrari's now legendary 1960s-era Berlinettas offered to customers in either touring or racing configurations.

Customers had the option of three Weber carburetors (with which the GTB was homologated for competition by the FIA) or a phalanx of six Weber 40 DCN/3s, endowing the engine with a brake horsepower capacity approaching 300. There was also a choice of construction, offering a combination of steel and aluminum or all-alloy body work, the

The Colombo-designed, sixty-degree, two-cam 275 GTB V12 had a swept volume of 3,285.7 cubic centimeters (273.8 cc per cylinder), and an output of 280 horsepower at 7,500 revolutions per minute.

GTB/C. Stylish Campagnolo 14-inch cast alloy wheels, re-creating the design used on the 1963 Tipo 156 Formula One cars, were standard, with the traditional Borrani wire wheels offered as an option.

The historian Dean Batchelor noted in the *Illustrated Ferrari Buyer's Guide*, "The 275 series marked the progressive change in Ferrari design philosophy from thinly disguised racers to comfortable and luxurious transportation vehicles. Because of the chassis changes—primarily the four-wheel independent suspension—the 275s were not only faster, but more comfortable than their predecessors."

Powered by a Colombo-designed sixty-degree V12 with a swept volume of 3,286 cubic centimeters (77 x 58.8 millimeter bore x stroke) and dispensing 280 horsepower at 7,600 revolutions per minute with the triple Weber carburetors, the 275 GTB was the ultimate expression of Ferrari's ideology: a road car suitable for racing that gave up little, if anything, to purebred competition models. With that in mind, Ferrari also offered a limited number of 275 GTB/C *competizione* (about a dozen) stripped for out-and-out racing, equipped with a dry sump engine and lighter weight sheet metal body work.

Exactly two years after the introduction of the 275 GTB, an even more powerful four-cam version made its world debut at the Paris Motor Show.

Ferrari was seldom first to introduce technical innovations. After all, Jaguar had been offering a double overhead camshaft engine in their production and competition cars since the late 1940s. Ferrari had been content to offer a single overhead cam engine (albeit a V12) until the early 1960s. By that time, more and more European road cars were appearing with four-cam engines beneath their hoods, not only Jaguar but Aston Martin and, in Italy, Alfa Romeo, Maserati, and a new marque, Lamborghini. Enzo was more or less being compelled by the competition to build a double overhead cam engine. However, if he was going to join in the fray, it would be on his own terms.

The 275 GTB four-cam was derived from the 3.3- and 4.0-liter engines that had powered the 275 and 330 P2 prototypes of the 1965 racing season, engines that were themselves derivatives of Colombo designs dating as far back as 1957. It was change, but not for the sake of change. It is interesting to note that between the first Ferrari twelve-cylinder 125 model of 1947 and the 275 GTB of 1964, that is

Far left:
Ferrari addressed the needs of its racing clientele with the 275 GTB/C or GTB *Competizione*, first offered in spring 1966. While the GTB/C retained the general appearance of the GTB, mechanically the differences were really quite radical. Note that the hood of the two-cam GTB does not have the raised power bulge that distinguishes the GTB/4 models at a glance.

to say over a seventeen-year career, Ferrari's sixty-degree V12 had gained more than 140 percent in specific power! Never before had Ferrari offered such a competition-oriented road car to the public: double overhead cams, dry sump lubrication, six twin-throat Weber carburetors, and 300 horsepower at 8,000 revolutions per minute.

The new four-cam engine was introduced in a revised 275 GTB body at the October 1966 Paris Motor Show. The prototype GTB/4, with chassis number 8769 GT and engine 8769 GT, was designed by Pininfarina and built (as were nearly all 275 GT bodies) by Sergio Scaglietti.

Sergio Pininfarina's exotic styling for the 275 GTB and GTB/4 had captured with great success the better elements of the compe-

The GTB/C models were fitted with the external quick fuel filler.

tition-built 250 GTO, as well as, at the rear, the styling of the GTB Lusso. The 275 GTB body had everything one could dream of in a road car, a long, plunging hood; small, oval radiator intake; streamlined, covered headlights; pronounced hood bulge; truncated rear; and fastback roof line—all perfectly harmonized to the contour of the steeply inclined and sharply curved windshield.

The GTB/4 proved an incomparable dual-purpose sports car that could challenge the ability of even the most skilled drivers. Commented the author Stanley Nowak, in his book *Ferrari—Forty Years on the Road*, "Like all of the best Ferraris, driving [the GTB/4] automatically focused one's concentration on getting the most out of it. It responded in kind. The more one puts into it, the more one gets out of it. Like most Ferraris, it is intended for serious drivers." The veteran race driver and former World Driving Champion Phil Hill described it as "like a boulevard version of the GTO."

While there are enthusiasts who will argue the point, the majority will agree that the 275 GTB and GTB/4 were the best-looking Berlinetta body styles ever produced by Ferrari, despite differing opinions about the 250 GTO and Berlinetta Lusso. Of the four-cam models, only about 280 examples were built. The rarest of all 275 GTB/4 models, however, were not Berlinettas, nor were they entirely built by Ferrari. These were the NART Spyders, the most controversial Ferrari ever built.

In *My Terrible Joys*, Enzo barely mentioned Chinetti's name, yet without him, it is unlikely Enzo Ferrari would have had much to write about. History will remember Chinetti, who succumbed to a heart ailment in 1994, shortly after celebrating his ninety-third birthday, as the man who truly built the Ferrari legend. As a dealer and importer, Chinetti understood the American market far better than Enzo. To please his customers, Luigi would not only challenge Il Commendatore's decisions but at times would have special Ferrari models produced at his own expense!

The North American Racing Team was to be an independent arm of the Scuderia Ferrari that would, on occasion, also represent the factory when Enzo Ferrari decided not to enter events under his own name. Over the years, NART became one of the most illustrious acronyms in American motor sports and a virtual who's who of legendary race drivers: Mario Andretti, Dan Gurney, Masten Gregory, Pedro and Ricardo Rodriguez, Paul O'Shea, Richie Ginther, Phil Hill, Stirling Moss, Bob Bondurant, Sam Posey, Jim Kimberly, Brian Redman, and Denise McCluggage. In the twenty-six years between 1956 and 1982, NART campaigned in more than two hundred races with more than 150 different drivers, including Luigi Chinetti, Jr.

Because of their friendship, Ferrari had granted Chinetti the right to use the Cavallino Rampante emblem as part of the NART insignia; however, all the decisions regarding the team were Chinetti's, and he often found himself at odds with Ferrari. They were two very stubborn men heading at times in the same direction and, at others, quite the opposite way.

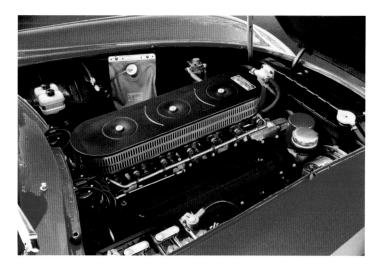

The 275 GTB/C engine had high-lift camshafts, 250 LM valves, reinforced pistons, a special crankshaft, and new Weber 40 DFI 3 carburetors. Built solely as a competition car, the GTB/C was equipped with a dry sump engine lubrication system and a separate oil reservoir.

The development of the NART Spyder in 1967 was the culmination of one of Chinetti and Ferrari's most famous disagreements. To Luigi, Spyders and convertibles were not interchangeable designs. Each had a well-defined purpose. When Chinetti had been a race driver, Spyders were open competition models like the 166 MM he had piloted to win Le Mans, cars that had no windows or tops, whereas a convertible had a folding top and windup windows. The fact that the differences were becoming less defined by the late 1950s was one reason Chinetti had pressed Ferrari into building the 250 GT Spyder California in 1958, and then the SWB version in 1960. Both examples sold well in the United States.

By 1964, the Ferrari production car line had been divided into four models: first the lavish 500 Superfast, continuing the luxury image Ferrari had established in the early 1960s with the 410 and

400 Superamericas, then the sleek 330 GT 2+2, and the stunning 275 GTB and GTB/C Berlinettas. But at the end of the line was the passionless 275 GTS, a Spyder in name only. It was built atop the GTB chassis but with an entirely different style body. This was a much more conservative styling concept that retained none of the exquisite lines penned by Sergio Pininfarina for the 275 GTB. To Chinetti, calling the 275 GTS a Spyder was a sheer corruption of the word and, in terms of its spirit and intent, an unworthy replacement for the Spyder Californias, with which he had achieved so much success in the U.S. market.

Enzo simply had no desire to build another special model for Chinetti's American market. He believed the 275 GTS was enough. If it had been regarded as a Cabriolet, perhaps it might have been, but the demand from Chinetti's customers was for an open racing version of the 275 GTB/4. Thus, Chinetti took it upon himself to build it without Ferrari. Luigi Jr. had actually proposed to his father the idea of building a Spyder based on the new 275 GTB/4 Berlinetta, arguably the car Maranello should have been building instead of the ignoble 275 GTS. To accomplish this task, the Chinettis turned to Enzo's principal coachbuilder, Sergio Scaglietti, commissioning the carrozzeria to build a series of competition Spyders out of Berlinetta models, exclusively for Chinetti Motors and NART. Scaglietti was an artist when it came to converting Berlinettas into Spyders and what emerged from the Modena coachbuilder's palette was a hand-built masterpiece.

Equipped with a four-cam V12 breathing through six Weber 40 DCN 17 carburetors, and delivering up to 330 horsepower at 8,000 revolutions per minute, the renamed 275 GTS/4 models were built atop a revised Tipo 596 all-independently suspended chassis, with the engine, prop-shaft tube, and transaxle all rigidly mounted along the frame, as on the new Ferrari 330 GTC.

From the exterior, any four-cam model was easily distinguished from the standard 275 GTB two-cam by a central power bulge in the hood. It was also obvious whenever a driver applied substantial pressure to the throttle pedal—the GTB/4 and GTS/4 could move from rest to 60 miles per hour in 6.7 seconds and reach a top speed in excess of 150 miles per hour.

The 275 GTB had been the first Ferrari road car to offer four-wheel independent suspension. The GTB/4 would be the first equipped with a double-overhead-camshaft engine. Not what you could call a significant change in the model, at least from appearances, but from behind the wheel, the GTB/4 had a character that clearly set it apart from its single-overhead-cam predecessor. Although it looked nearly identical, except for a prominent hood bulge, the GTB/4 offered owners a 300-horsepower double-overhead cam V12.

The styling of the 275 GTB and GTB/4 was an evolution of the 250 GTO and GT Berlinetta Lusso, the influences of which can be seen in this rear three-quarter view.

Below:
The 275 GTB/4 engine was another Colombo-based sixty-degree V12 design utilizing double overhead camshafts on each bank. Compression ratio was 9.2:1, with fuel delivered by six Weber twin-choke downdraft carburetors. Output for the four-cam was rated at 300 horsepower at 8,000 revolutions per minute.

The redesigned 275 GTs were delivered from Scaglietti to Chinetti Motors and sold exclusively in North America. Although Maranello scarcely acknowledged the existence of the 275 GTS/4 NART Spyder, it was to become one of Ferrari's most sought after models, and today many copies exist, cars that started life as Berlinettas and ended up converted into Spyders.

The first car arrived stateside in February 1967. Stamped with chassis number 09437, it was painted giallo solare (sun yellow) and contrasted with a rich black leather interior. To give his new car a proper introduction, Chinetti had the first NART Spyder entered in the 12 Hours of Sebring. To drive, he selected two women, Pinkie Rollo and Denise McCluggage. The two had proven themselves in an OSCA at Sebring in the late 1950s, and McCluggage had won her class, finishing tenth overall at Sebring in 1961

with a Ferrari Berlinetta. However, while driving the NART Spyder at Sebring, McCluggage would encounter a driver's worst nightmare, a disorganized pit crew. Perhaps they were out of step because, at this race, Luigi Chinetti was not present to supervise.

"Luigi was a scoundrel or a champion, depending in part on how much money you had and how much talent as a racing driver," says McCluggage. "Truth be told, Luigi had a knack for manipulating his wealthy clients into subsidizing those less blessed with monetary riches but with keener hand, eye and right foot coordination. Some of his rich Ferrari clients caught on and willingly collaborated in support of Luigi's racing program. Some waxed indignant at the heavy cost for Ferrari maintenance and bad-mouthed Luigi around the car world (Luigi shrugged his classic Italian shrug). And some just kept paying. They might themselves log only a few laps in the race car they had paid so much to prepare for Le Mans or Sebring, but they belonged. Their helmets rested on the pit wall along with those of Phil Hill, Portago, Pedro Rodriguez, etc.; they were part of Luigi's NART—the North American Racing Team," explains McCluggage with a sense of pride in her voice.

Though Luigi Chinetti might often be described as a Ferrari distributor and dealer, and the man who brought Ferrari to the

United States, he was far more than that. "Without Luigi," contends McCluggage, "it's possible that a disheartened Enzo Ferrari would never have returned to building racing cars when World War II ended." History knows that Ferrari did return to building race cars, and it was the road cars that paid for them. "Luigi introduced the cars to France and to the U.S. and found rich people to buy them and talented people to race them," says McCluggage. "And he ably juggled the two to assure Ferrari's progression to iconic status in the New World. He even found Ferrari's first American champion, Phil Hill.

"So some clients were miffed at being used, the ones whose souls were blind to Luigi's vision of finding promising drivers to race the cars he had on that dim Christmas Eve in 1946 talked Enzo Ferrari into building. For Luigi the world was in balance when good drivers drove good cars and won races. His purpose in life was to make that happen. He was uniquely able to do it."

Built on the greatest Ferrari platform of its time, the chassis for the NART Spyder was the 275 GTB/4 Berlinetta. Redesigning the stunning 275 GTB/4 Berlinetta into a Spyder was a task few would have undertaken, but Sergio Scaglietti took the Pininfarina fastback and cut the roof cleanly away, leaving the flowing rear fender line intact and blended perfectly into a rear-deck lid.

McCluggage, an award-winning journalist, author, and race driver, became specifically aware of Luigi Chinetti in her first race in a Jaguar XK140 at the Montgomery, New York, airport in 1957. She recalls, "He was smiling broadly at me and waggling my elbow saying: 'Pro-BOB-ly' (he always said it like that), 'Pro-BOB-ly we should get you into a Ferrari.' I didn't understand the significance of that then because I was only vaguely aware of his racing history—with Alfa Romeo where he and Ferrari were team drivers, his records set at Montlhéry, his Mexican road race experiences and his three victo-

ries at Le Mans, more than anyone else could claim for a long time to come. Nor did I know of his reputation for discovering and nurturing racing talent. I had been well and truly complimented and it had passed by my ears.

"I did get into a Ferrari several years later, a short-wheel-based 250 GT Scaglietti-bodied Berlinetta. It was dark blue and had been raced at Le Mans in 1960. How could I even think of a Ferrari? I was a freelance journalist living in a five-flight walk-up in New York's Greenwich Village. The place was so small I could stand in the center of my

When Luigi Chinetti formed the North American Racing Team in 1956, Enzo Ferrari granted him permission to use the Cavallino Rampante emblem, which Chinetti flanked with a stylized American flag and the NART acronym.

kitchen and touch all four of its walls. My book shelves were scavenged bricks and boards. But thanks to Luigi and Briggs Cunningham the unimaginable became reality and I owned a Ferrari. It was not only my only car, it was my only thing. At the time a used Ferrari was $9,000. Upkeep? Someone was probably paying but I never got a bill.

"The Berlinetta came into my hands in time for Sebring in March, 1961. That was the plan. My co-driver was a jazz musician, saxophonist Allen Eager, who had raced before only in his fantasies. It was my wont to indulge men's fantasies insofar as I was able so I asked him if he wanted to drive with me at Sebring. Oh yes he did. And the process of acquisition was set in motion. I saw to it that

Allen got some practice at a deserted Lime Rock and in a small race at Vineland, New Jersey. He had a knack for driving, one that transferred well to the race course though not all do.

"At Sebring we finished tenth overall, winning our class and the Grand Touring category. First in GT drew the same in prize money ($2,000) as first overall which was won by Phil Hill and Olivier Gendebien in a factory Testa Rossa. Before the money could burn a hole in our pocket we used it to fly the Ferrari to Europe and enter the 1000 K's at the Nürburgring. Racing, like most everything else, was simpler then. And affordable enough to be engaged by whim.

The first NART Spyder, equipped with U.S. instrumentation, had a maximum speed, as tested by *Road & Track* magazine, of 150 miles per hour. The interior of the NART Spyder was straightforward in Ferrari tradition: no superfluous trim, just the necessary instruments and a hand-sewn leather dashboard. Seats were upholstered in black leather. The color scheme was a vivid contrast to the soft yellow exterior of the first car. Note the large metal-gated shifter used on the 275 series.

"I had the entrant of record at Sebring for the Berlinetta. But it could just as easily have been a NART entry. The North American Racing Team was never a team like racing understands teams today. It was more like a pick-up basketball game at the corner playground. But, mind you, in a seriously competitive neighborhood. For each race, Luigi would improvise his entries according to who was available, who he wanted to give some seat time and who had deep pockets. He might pair a promising or even proven driver with a moneyed client who might or might not get a satisfying stint at the wheel. It took careful planning: the idea was to win which meant the best driver would be longer at the wheel. But the client whose largesse might be needed for a future race must not feel short-changed. Luigi was a master at this juggling act," recalls McCluggage.

"NART was thus any entry Luigi made with any drivers he nominated. He might have as many as seven or eight entries in any one race. I was, and I'm sure others were too, a NART driver without really thinking about it," says McCluggage. "We were simply driving a car that involved Luigi. NART, it seems to me, has taken on the structure of a real racing team only in retrospect. Years after the fact people who are given to imposing order on past events and calling it *History* have compiled lists of all the drivers who ever drove a NART entry. I was on the list and seeing my name there realized I was a NART driver. The list is an impressive one. A few of the names on it: Phil Hill, Dan Gurney, Stirling Moss, Richie

The Tipo 226 V12 used in the NART was based upon the P2 prototype racing engines that had been used by the factory team in 1965. The dual overhead camshafts were an obvious major design change from the previous 3.3-liter GTB. The revised V12 delivered up to 330 horsepower at 8,000 revolutions per minute and breathed through six Weber 40 DCN 17 carburetors, which are shown here. Rarely does one see a picture of this engine with the carburetors exposed.

The firewall identification plate on the first NART Spyder still identifies the car as a 275 GTB/4, i.e., a Berlinetta.

Ginther, John Surtees, the Rodriguez brothers, Jim Hall, Mario Andretti, A. J. Foyt, etc."

Denise's best-known NART ride was that first 275 GTS/4, although technically it wasn't a NART entry! At Sebring the previous year Mario Andretti, driving for NART, had been involved in an incident at the turn known as Webster's, in which two spectators died. Threatened lawsuits kept Luigi from entering the race the next year. Indeed, the risk of litigation kept him out of Florida entirely. "He turned the Spyder over to me (I think I may have paid a dollar for it) and I entered the car in the Twelve Hours of Sebring," says McCluggage. "At the time I was living at the Sugarbush ski area in northern Vermont so I took 'NART', knocked the bar out of the A, flipped it over and voila: NVRT: the Northern Vermont Racing Team. Did I say things were simpler in those days?

"But we had a sponsor, a rarity then. Citgo had bought a book I had written called *Are You a Woman Driver?* to give as a premium, like steak knives, to purchasers of full tanks of gas. (The gas station experience was different then, too.) And Citgo extended the relationship to include sponsoring the 275 GTS/4 at Sebring. I think that involved their paying Luigi $6,000.

"Nonetheless without Luigi present at the race course we had a rather haphazard crew arrangement. At least to begin with." As the race progressed the five other Ferraris entered fell out and that left McCluggage's pale yellow convertible as the only prancing horse on the track. With five cars out, the idled Ferrari mechanics

Denise McCluggage was one of the first professional women race drivers in America, and the first to race the 275 GTS/4 NART Spyder. Her first turn behind the wheel of the new four-cam Spyder was at Sebring in 1967. (*Photograph by Dave Friedman*)

all migrated to McCluggage's pits hoping to help avoid total erasure of the marque. "I don't know if they were there for the disastrous pit stop in which all four wheels were removed but only three could be found to replace them! The car went out to circulate with worn rubber while another wheel was outfitted with a new tire and then was called back in. Maybe that extra stop stole enough time to lose us the class victory—it was close—but then the Shelby American that won had an added incentive, or so their head mechanic told me later. 'We didn't want to get beat by no women!'

"The yellow Spyder was the first of a proposed 25 such Pininfarina convertibles that Luigi commissioned Scaglietti to build for the U.S. market. Only ten were actually made," says McCluggage. "Our race car was one of only two with aluminum bodywork and the only one known to be raced.

"Enzo didn't like open cars and Luigi did. Nor did Enzo like yellow cars and Luigi did. Luigi told me with a laugh: 'He say, 'You make a taxi cab!' But Luigi believed that he would have won Le Mans four times instead of three if his car had been more readily visible to the scorers. He thinks his dark car was missed in the rain and gloom on one lap, a lap that would have meant another victory. A yellow car, he believed, would have been seen and noted."

After Sebring the NART Spyder went on to a short movie career with Steve McQueen (who bought the sixth NART Spyder) and Faye

d'Elegance. Coincidentally McCluggage was the guest Grand Marshall of the event and presented the trophy. "An occasion for some eyes misty with nostalgia," she says. Another coincidence McCluggage reveals is that before Steve McQueen had left New York to become a TV and movie star, "we two had been an item in Greenwich Village where we both had MG-TCs.

"Later this storied car's sale financed the birth of Brumos Porsche in Jacksonville, or so I was told by Bob Snodgrass, a Brumos principal. And in 2005 at Pebble Beach the car drew the top bid for any car in any auction held that week—3.6 million dollars. I drove the car up on the platform with Luigi Chinetti, Jr. as my passenger.

"Pro-BOB-ly Luigi Sr. would have smiled and shrugged."

Right after the race at Sebring, Chinetti sent the NART Spyder off to *Road & Track* magazine for testing. The article appearing in the September 1967 issue reported an impressive top speed of 155 miles per hour and the velocity at the end of a 14.7-second standing start quarter-mile as 99 miles per hour. *R & T* proclaimed it "the most satisfying sports car in the world."

Although ten examples hardly constitute "production," among Ferraris it is a respectable number, especially for a car that the factory had no intention of building. Fortunately, thanks to Luigi Chinetti's vision of a proper Spyder, today we have the 275 GTS/4.

As a race driver turned importer turned race team manager, Luigi Chinetti was a master at getting the most out of his drivers and his cars. Chinetti is seen here at Daytona in 1963 with driver Pedro Rodriguez.

Dunaway in the 1968 version of *The Thomas Crown Affair*. It was painted a more camera-friendly burgundy for the occasion. And then years later in 1987 following a Shelton restoration in Florida—and a return to its original yellow—the NART Spyder won best-in-show at the Ferrari Club of America's 25th anniversary Concours

The Chinettis and NART
By R. L. Wilson

Because I was a keen admirer of both automobile racing and Ferraris from the 1950s—though I did not possess a driver's license until age twenty-five—my circumstances led to a close friendship with the NART racing team and the Chinetti family, Luigi Chinetti, Sr., and Luigi, Jr., affectionately known as Coco.

As a Ferrari owner (my first was a 246GT Dino), I brought the car down from my home in Hadlyme (east of New Haven) for servicing at Chinetti Motors. On one occasion, Marion, Luigi's wife of many years, and a lovely lady, asked me if I ever drove the Dino in the rain (she didn't approve). On another, Miles Davis's road manager had brought in the jazz trumpet legend's white 246GT for service. The incredible clientele of the Chinettis for Ferraris, and for other high-performance machines, was one of the reasons Enzo Ferrari had struck up an arrangement with Luigi Sr. in 1946. Luigi told me they had been friends since he was about nineteen years of age!

Once Luigi sold me a Formula Two Ferrari, one of five he had imported in the late 1960s. This magnificent machine was the centerpiece of my Hadlyme office for a couple of years. I remember when the car was wheeled out of his Greenwich showroom; he turned away and went into his office. That beautiful machine had been a fixture on display for years, and he had an emotional attachment to it. Luigi felt that the finest of performance cars, the racers, had souls. Over the years, until days before Luigi Sr.'s death, I had frequent opportunities to hear a considerable number of stories from father and son about their adventures in racing and in dealing with not only the ultimate in sports cars but with the ultimate in clients.

In 1981, '82, and '83 I was one of the sponsors of the Chinetti entry at Le Mans. Contributing to the race effort and costs, supporters could stay at the country house property rented exclusively for the team and its sponsors, in a quiet, sedate part of Le Mans. You ate with the team, traveled to the track with the Chinetti entourage, and had the complement of credentials.

Each year the Chinettis entered a 512BB, specially modified by the factory, and with sponsors—among others, Cartier. With a photography pass I could freely enter the pits, and walk around the track (with cars speeding by at more than two hundred miles an hour; I doubt that insurance today would permit those long walks). You could cross the track at the end of the Mulsanne Straight—as long as the safety marshal waved you over.

Le Mans became like old home week for both Luigi Sr. and Luigi Jr. As official photographer, I would take thousands of pictures. Luigi Sr. particularly would often ask to be photographed with old friends, some he had met during his first race as the Alfa Romeo representative in Paris, in the early 1930s.

For the 1982 race, a fabulous dinner was set up at a monastery in Le Mans, celebrating the fiftieth anniversary of Luigi's first Le Mans win (in an Alfa). This was a major event, attended by every dignitary and celebrated with the kind of party that Old World Europeans can do without compare.

Later that year several of NART's drivers were present at New York City's Wave Hill estate for a fiftieth-anniversary dinner sponsored by

Road & Track magazine, again commemorating Chinetti's first victory at Le Mans and his remarkable automotive career. Among the guests were Dan Gurney, Phil Hill, Carroll Shelby, Jim Kimberly, Denise McCluggage, Bob Grossman, and more than one hundred fellow racers, clients, and old friends (the likes of Zora Arkus-Duntov, Rene Dreyfus, John Weitz, and Bill Ruger). Among those who sent their best wishes were Mario Andretti, Richie Ginther, Janet Guthrie, and Stirling Moss. Remembered by all were the late Harry Schell, Graham Hill, the Rodriguez brothers, and the Marquis de Portago—all NART alumni. Like many others, the marquis' racing career was launched by Luigi Chinetti (in the bar at the Ritz Hotel, Paris, Luigi persuaded de Portago that auto racing was more exciting than horses).

Arno Werner, the renowned bookbinder for Harvard's Houghton Library rare book collection, bound a beautiful scrapbook in leather. Every guest signed the book, and a collection of photographs and press clippings was part of the volume. Its presentation was done by me, after an introduction by Luigi Jr., as one of the two masters of ceremony.

As the years passed, Luigi Jr. moved to Lyme and we were neighbors—often watching Grand Prix races on a large-screen satellite TV hookup in my office, and getting together socially and occasionally at Ferrari club meets or racing events. Luigi's fiftieth birthday was at my Hadlyme property. Several pages in my guest book are inscribed by the more than seventy-five longtime friends who attended, including Morley Safer of *60 Minutes*. The presence of Luigi Sr. prevented the otherwise inevitable mega food fight—something for which Coco has developed a worldwide reputation.

When authoring *The World of Beretta* many years later, I learned that the Ferrari factory had a shotgun shooting team, which from time to time would visit Beretta's main factory in Gardone, Val Trompia. Ugo Gussalli Beretta is himself a car enthusiast, and had met Ferrari.

On my first visit to Beretta, when I was under contract with Random House to author the book, Luigi Jr. was along, as were the author Dennis Adler and our mutual friend Steve Fjestad (publisher and author of the *Blue Book of Gun Values*). On that occasion we spent a day at the Ferrari factory and were allowed to drive on the Fiorano track the latest models of cars (I as a passenger with Luigi—a highly experienced and expert white-knuckle driver).

As I traveled with both Chinettis over the years, it became clear that each had his particular lifestyle and joie de vivre. The Chinetti-NART story still needs to be told. The Chinetti collection of more than ten thousand photographs, trophies, and memorabilia helps to document a unique and breathtaking panorama of the competition automobile from the 1920s through modern times. Luigi Sr. told me of Coco racing against Gilles Villeneuve, in a Formula event in Canada, in which (driving equal cars) Coco bested Villeneuve. Luigi Sr. was convinced that Coco could have been a World Formula One Champion. That Coco was an only child had to have been a factor in dissuading Luigi Jr. from the intense dedication that kind of career would have demanded. Anyone who knows Coco recognizes a depth of automobile knowledge that is unique. I have always felt privileged to have been a part of the NART story, if only from behind the lens of a camera.

When R. L. (Larry) Wilson first met the Chinettis, in the early 1970s, he had already been a car buff since boyhood. An inveterate collector, he saved everything he could and kept notes of numerous trips, races, cars, and stories from both Luigi Sr. and Coco. Photographs at the Daytona 24 Hours (1979) and from Le Mans (1978, 1982, and 1983) were thanks to press credentials obtained by the Chinettis and requested by Wilson's editor at Simon & Schuster, Michael Korda. Working mainly in color print film, but occasionally in black and white, Wilson shot thousands of pictures, and a set of the best prints was then given to the Chinettis partly to encourage their writing a book of their own.

Early design of the NART-Ferrari logo, approved by Ferrari and unique to NART, at *upper left,* ultimate evolution, at *lower left,* to the right of the Ferrari logo silk tie. The prancing horse tile used at Ferrari factory sites in Italy, as well as by the Chinettis in their Greenwich and New York showrooms.

Early black-and-whites at *left* document Luigi Sr.'s friendship with the Formula One Bugatti racer Rene Dreyfus and early racing and sports car pursuits during the World War II period in the United States.

Left center, the Hotel Fini, the customary place to stay when at Ferrari factory visits.

Lower left, black-and-white of 1964 Formula One car (blue and white with NART logo) at Watkins Glen, John Surtees at the wheel, entered for Ferrari by the NART team. The casual portrait photo of Luigi to *right* of the Formula One was a favorite, taken in front of his home, holding a model of the victorious 1949 Le Mans car, the 166 MM Number 22, by the journalist, photographer, and Chinetti friend Tom Burnside. Book at *left* showing Chinetti in the pits at that race is *Ferraris at Le Mans,* by Dominique Pascal, signed to Wilson with a display of Chinetti wit by Luigi.

Miniature car of the 365 GTB/4 Daytona of Coco and Bob Grossman, which won first in class at Le Mans 1974, after which sales of that model took off. Model of the 1965 Jochen Rindt and Maston Gregory 275 LM salutes the 1965 NART victory at Le Mans. Model of the 1933 Alfa Romeo 2300 of Nuvolari-Compagnoni, symbolic of 1932, 1933, and 1934 competitions at Le Mans of Chinetti, who won in Alfas in 1932 and '34, and was beaten by Nuvolari in 1933.

Above 365 GTB/4 Daytona black-and-white showing the NASCAR chief Bill France, Sr., and entourage, at the 1979 Daytona 24 Hours, with Luigi in front of his boxer entry, Number 68. Drawings by Coco at *top center* (to *right* of NART driver Gregg Young trackside in sweater). The car crashed on the high banking, and Wilson photographed it extensively for NART's insurance claims.

The automotive journalist and racer Paul Frere and Luigi Jr. with Daytona at Le Mans, to *left* of snapshots of Luigi Sr. and his wife, Marion, at Wilson's Hadlyme (Connecticut) home; the 1968 Ferrari Formula Two purchased from the Chinettis in the 1970s.

At *center,* next to a crashed 308GTB, Coco at the Ferrari factory; at *right,* Engineer Florini, who worked with the Chinettis in the late 1970s and early '80s preparing factory cars for racing. Wilson's son Peter, whom Coco termed his "aide-de-camp," to *left,* with a youthful Ferrari engineer.

Above, Le Mans press pass for 1978, the Chinettis again with Paul Frere, keen on Ferraris and a longtime Chinetti friend and colleague. *Above,* Wilson's son Peter with the 1980 Le Mans entry number 74. Boxer number 72 was the entrant for 1982. Above Peter and number 74, Amedee Polledri of Paris, with Philippe le Rouvillois of Monaco, both old friends of the Chinettis, who were regulars at the Le Mans events.

"American Commendatore" was the title of Pete Lyons's cover-story tribute to then ninety-three-year-old Luigi in the *Autoweek* issue August 22, 1994. Chinetti was "the man who first represented the Prancing Horse in America, who passionately waved its banner on the track and skillfully sold its image to rich, Ferrari-feverish Americans, sometimes in the face of Enzo's enmity." The Denise McCluggage article "Coco Is Best Served in Italy" appeared in *Autoweek,* December 12, 1988, describing an inspired design and manufacturing project of Coco, with Scaglietti, of a then unnamed Modena-built but Coco-designed super exotic sports car—and of an ambitious 12-liter, twelve-cylinder dream machine, the Chinetti Doppia Dodici.

Below, front end of Le Mans number 72 NART boxer at *upper right,* Luigi sitting on a Niki Lauda Formula One wheel in his home garage; the yellow NART coupe, a Chinetti design project of which there were numerous others over the years, many of them designed by Coco. These two rare machines were among a select group that Luigi kept at his home rather than at the showrooms on West Putnam Avenue.

Center right at bottom, black-and-white showing a 288 GTO at a restaurant near Maranello, photographed by Coco, who gave Wilson a 168-mile-an-hour ride up to Gardone, Brescia (Val Trompia), from the Ferrari factory—a four-hour trip in but forty-five minutes, to visit the gunmaker Aldo Uberti and his beautiful daughter Maria.

Top right, both Juan Manuel Fangio and the designer John Weitz were among the legion of friends and colleagues who figured in the careers of the Chinettis and the long reign of NART.

There were many tributes to Luigi as the years passed by, among them a fiftieth-anniversary dinner at Le Mans, 1982, celebrating his first win there in 1932. The gala event at Wave Hill, also in 1982, organized by *Road & Track* magazine, drew more than 150 attendees. A highlight of the evening was a photograph made in front of the mansion, with all who attended. The "Profile" article, by Jonathan Thompson, was published in the *Road & Track* issue of October 1982.

Luigi Sr.'s death in August 1994 came just before the Pebble Beach Concours d'Elegance and the attendant Laguna Seca vintage racing weekend.

The 1996 Ferrari Club of America's tribute to NART and the Chinetti legacy proved a well-attended, popular, and timely event. Coco was a featured speaker on the final evening.

Bottom right, helping to celebrate the legacy of Ferrari and Chinetti, and the magic of the motorcar, are the collectors Arturo Keller and Bob Lee, at Pebble Beach. Lee is the owner of Chinetti's 1949 Le Mans-winning 166 MM. *(Photograph montage by Douglas Sandburg)*

Between them spanning more than eighty years of dedication to the magical world of performance automobiles, the Chinettis shared a knowledge and experience rivaled by few. Luigi Sr. enjoyed cars as a boy in his uncle's garage in Milan and had met Ferrari by the time he was nineteen. They were very close in age and developed one of the classic collaborations in the history of motor sports, as well as automaking and distribution.

In contrast to the first collage, this collection concentrates primarily on the Chinettis in racing, with Berlinetta Boxers entered into Daytona 1979 (number 68) and at Le Mans in 1980 (number 74) and 1982 (number 72). At *top center,* the pits at Le Mans, in an uncharacteristically quiet repose.

A few shots relate to the period before World War II, such as the deck chair racers onboard the *Comte di Savoia* in May 1940. From *left,* Luigi, Rene Dreyfus, Mrs. Le Begue, and Harry Schell. The Chinetti and Dreyfus voyage to America is covered in detail in *My Two Lives: Race Driver to Restaurateur,* by Dreyfus with Beverly Rae Kimes. At *lower left,* attending the New York World's Fair, 1939, at the Ford Pavilion, with Rene Le Begue, Harry Schell, Rene Dreyfus (all except Luigi smoking). *Upper left, above,* Le Mans photo of number 22 166 MM at Indianapolis, with the Maserati entered with Dreyfus as driver, 1940. *Above,* the monastery in Le Mans at which the fiftieth-anniversary dinner was held honoring Luigi, 1982. To *right,* ticket to the Ferrari Museum, Modena.

Lower left, one of the most detailed histories of NART and Ferrari in America was Albert R. Bochroch's article in the 1975 *Automobile Quarterly*/Dutton book *Ferrari: The Man, the Machines.* The inscribed image shows Chinetti in the pits at Le Mans, c. 1961.

Right center, Ferrarisima, a limited, numbered, and signed edition of five thousand copies, number 21 (published 1994), included a tribute to Luigi titled "When Ferraris Were White and Blue," by R. L. Wilson.

Bottom center, the Chinettis with Phil Hill, 1982. Under the *Ferraris at Le Mans* book by Dominique Pascal, a photograph of Coco with Francois Secard, a longtime mechanic with the Chinettis who worked several races as part of team NART.

Far right, Coco with Dennis Adler (right) and the author/publisher Steve Fjestad at the Ferrari factory, Maranello. The crashed 246GT Dino and 308GTB were Wilson's, the former totaled by him braking down from sixty-five miles per hour to avoid a near head-on collision on a Connecticut River country road. In the process the steering wheel was bent as (without seat belts) he held on to prevent heading through the windshield. The 308 was crashed by Wilson's wife, Charlotte, into

a creek bed (she was then three months pregnant with their son Stephen, today a car buff) the day the machine was to be at Chinetti Motors for a fifteen-hundred-mile checkup!

The Hotel Fini brochure included, for many years, a lounge photo showing Wilson, his son Peter, and Coco, enjoying the ambiance of a preferred hotel while visiting the Ferrari factory.

Bottom right, Salvador Dali ashtray suggests a keen interest in art, both Chinettis, prone sometimes to take it in trade on cars.

Top right center, Luigi Sr., as Marshal of the 1982 Le Mans race, waves the flag at the start; the tremendous speed of the cars seems to be sucking the entourage onto the track. Wilson held on to Luigi to make sure he did not disappear into the thundering herd of powerful machines.

Left center, above a New York Yacht Club packet of soap, the charming hotel in Le Mans, leased for years by NART for its team, sponsors, and guests during race week. Among NYYC members was the racer Briggs Cunningham, an early patron, then rival, of the Chinettis and NART.

Top right, the author-publisher Michael Korda, to the right of "programme official," wrote letters to request press passes at Le Mans for Wilson in the hope of publishing the official history of NART and the Chinettis. To *right,* Luigi at the Le Mans pits, 4:00 PM, just at the start of the 1983 race. He was determined to remain trackside as long as the NART cars were still in the race.

Note drawings by Coco; drumsticks recall one of his many talents—music; he also pursued photography and was involved in films on NART and racing in the 1960s. *Top center,* one of Coco's custom designs, the

Michelotti, with one of the Le Mans officials at the wheel. Wilson and his then girlfriend Suzanne O'Sullivan are treated to a 170-mile-per-hour trip down Mulsanne in this machine, with Coco at the wheel.

Upper right, signatures of Luigi Sr. and Jr., and of Marion, taken from Wilson's guest book.

Luigi's dedication to cars, to performance, and to speed was such that he told Wilson his doctor had said he could still drive in competition at Le Mans. Should he have had a heart attack, he would still have been able to maneuver the car off the track! In the early 1980s, when driving with Wilson as a passenger from Maranello to Paris, Luigi kept a Ferrari 400 at about 175 miles per hour continuously, and made the trip in just over nine hours! It was necessary that he drive all the way since insurance on the car covered only him as the driver. The 400 hit a large bird with the windshield on Wilson's side while at 175 mph; that missile disappeared immediately; Luigi kept right on driving and didn't miss a beat. But it brought on yet another story—about the PanAmerican race in which a vulture was struck by a Mercedes 300 SL ahead of Luigi, then hit his car, going through the windshield: "There was blood and feathers everywhere!" That was always part of the pleasure with the Chinettis—they never forgot anything and were brimming with the most amazing stories of two incredible lives. *(Photograph montage by Douglas Sandburg)*

Enzo Ferrari and Bill Harrah

Ferrari Factory, Maranello, Italy May, 1961

One of the greatest patrons of the Cavallino Rampante was millionaire hotel and casino owner William Harrah. Harrah and Ferrari posed for this photo at the Maranello, Italy, factory in May 1961. Harrah's impact on promoting Ferraris through his own contacts and clientele proved significant.

Road Cars for America and the World

The influence of the Chinettis on Ferrari sales and notoriety in the United States led to the North American market becoming one of the most important for Ferrari's continued success. Thus, many of the cars built in the late 1960s, into the 1970s, and to this day, have been created with American buyers in mind.

While the Lusso had come closer to being a true touring car than any of its predecessors, and ideally suited to the American market, Ferrari had already undertaken development of a genuine luxury model with the 400 Superamerica, which was built concurrently with the Lusso through 1964. The 400 Superamerica was also designed by Pininfarina, drawing on several auto show styling themes from the early 1960s, including the sensational Superfast II shown at the Turin Motor Show in 1960.

The styling of the 400 Superamerica, which gave rise to the 500 Superfast in 1964, has been a subject of debate for decades among Ferrari owners and sports car enthusiasts. On one side there are the critics, who called the 400 Superamerica ugly and disproportionate; wrote one pundit, "cover up first the front, and then the back with your hand or a piece of paper, and they do not look like the same vehicle." On the other side were those who called it one of the most exciting designs of the era. Somewhere between the extremes was the truth, although the 500 Superfast was undeniably a better looking

With sleek, aerodynamic styling, the 500 Superfast was truly worthy of its name—originally coined by Pininfarina for a show car. The body design was based in part on the 250 GT Berlinetta Lusso and the Superfast's predecessor, the 400 Superamerica.

car, with softened body lines, a squared-off transom tail, uncovered headlights, and a more graceful rear pillar and backlight.

In creating the 500 Superfast, Sergio Pininfarina had retained the aesthetic lines of the *aerodynamico* coupes but refined and tailored the lines of the 500 more closely to those of the 250 GT Berlinetta Lusso, which had been a styling triumph for both Ferrari and Pininfarina.

The 500 Superfast made its debut at the Geneva Motor Show in March 1964. A larger, more luxurious, and more powerful replacement for the 400 Superamerica, it had beneath the hood a modified sixty-degree V12 based on both the Colombo and the Lampredi designs. Displacement was increased from the Superamerica's 3,967 to 4,962 cubic centimeters, to arrive at a cubic inch displacement that was highly regarded in America, 302 cubic inches (actually 302.7).

Pininfarina relied heavily upon established Ferrari styling cues when designing new models. The Superfast, for example, had fender louvers similar to the 400 Superamerica's, which were derived from the earlier 410 Superamerica. The fender lines have their origin in the Lusso. Says the designer, Sergio Pininfarina, "Creating a new design is not always an easy task. On one hand, if you are following too much of a traditional look, you risk repeating yourself and not being innovative enough. On the other hand, I think it is right that I resist the temptation to make every car I design extraordinary."

With the use of wood veneers to accent the instrument panel and center console, the interior of the 500 Superfast was the most luxurious of any Ferrari built up to that time.

This was accomplished by using the 108-millimeter (4.26-inch) bore centers of the 1950 Lampredi-designed long block sixty-degree V12 with the general mechanical layout of the big Colombo V12, thus creating a hybrid engine with 88-millimeter (3.46-inch) bore and 68-millimeter (2.68-inch) stroke.

The Lampredi design used in the 410 Superamerica series, produced from 1956 to 1959, had the same bore and stroke as the new 500 Superfast. The big Colombo V12, introduced with the 400 Superamerica, used a smaller bore of 77 millimeters (3.05 inches) and longer stroke of 71 millimeters (2.79 inches), displacing 3,967 cubic centimeters (242 cubic inches). With this momentary return to the older Lampredi dimensions for the 500 Superfast, engine output was now a robust 400 horsepower at 6,500 revolutions per minute, the same as it had been for the 1950s-era 410 Superamerica. Changing the engine's compression ratio was another assist in output. The Lampredi engine used 8.5:1 and delivered 340 horsepower at 6,000 rpm. The later engines, with 9:1 compression, produced the much vaunted 400 horsepower. The 500 Superfast had an 8.8:1 compression ratio, the

same as that of the Colombo-based 400 Superamerica, which had delivered only 340 horsepower at 7,000 rpm. It should also be noted that the early 400 Superamerica had a 9.8:1 compression ratio and produced the same 400 horsepower as the 500 Superfast but at a higher rpm. Both the Lampredi and Colombo engines used three twin-choke Weber downdraft carburetors.

In 1964 the 500 Superfast had the most powerful engine available in a passenger car. The first series, about twenty-five examples, used the four-speed, all-synchromesh transmission with electrically operated overdrive from the 400 Superamerica. The second series, an even dozen cars built from late 1965 to the end of production in 1966, were little changed but did include side louvers in the fenders and a five-speed, all-synchromesh gearbox, with direct drive in fourth gear.

The Superfast was built on a 2,650-millimeter (104.2-inch) wheelbase (50 millimeters longer than the 400 Superamerica LWB

A rear-deck design traditional on Ferrari Spyders such as the 330 GTS adapted surprisingly well to the coupe configuration of the 330 GTC, which actually preceded the 330 Spyder into production by six months.

Fender louvers became a Ferrari trademark after the 410 Superamerica of 1956. Pininfarina continually revised the design, which on the 330 GTC took on a very artistic appearance.

Top right:
Taking its interior styling cues from the 500 Superfast, the 330 GTC featured wood veneer on the dashboard, although leather was again applied to finish the center console. Power windows (switches on either side of the cigarette lighter) were one of many convenience features offered. This example was also equipped with air conditioning.

platform) with a 1,407-millimeter (55.5-inch) front and 1,397-millimeter (55.2-inch) rear track, both slightly wider than the 400. The suspension was of similar design: A-arms, coil springs, telescopic shock absorbers in front, and a live axle rear with semielliptic springs and telescopic shock absorbers. Other than the engine, mechanical specifications for the 500 Superfast were almost identical to those of the companion 330 GT, introduced in 1964.

The 500 Superfast was the most luxurious car Ferrari had built up to that time: the ultimate in front-engined Ferraris "for those who like the Rolls-Royce touch with their performance," as the historian Hans Tanner wrote in 1974. But no one summed up the

The 330 GTC utilized the same engine as the earlier 330 GT 2+2, a 300-horsepower Colombo-based V12 displacing 3,967 cubic centimeters (242 cubic inches). The cars were equipped with a five-speed, all-synchromesh transmission built in-unit with the differential.

Superamerica better than Antoine Prunet, who decreed that "Ferrari and Pininfarina had, without question, created quite well the Ferrari 'Royale.'"

Maranello's flagship coupe was luxuriously upholstered in buttery leather and accented with hand-rubbed wood trim on the instrument panel, dashboard, and center console. Power windows were a standard feature, as was an AM/FM push-button radio.

When construction of the 500 Superfast concluded with the thirty-seventh car in the series, it brought an end to limited-production Ferrari coupes and Berlinettas. The Superfast and its kin were gone forever and with them a chapter in Italian sports car history that will never be forgotten.

Ferrari's advances in luxury GTs reached an all-time high for the 1960s with the 1966 introduction of the 330 GTC and GTS models. The GTC made its debut in March at the Geneva show. The 330 GTC was the ultimate Ferrari hybrid, utilizing the chassis of the 275 GTB, the engine of the 330 GT 2+2 (introduced in 1964), and a body design by Pininfarina that combined the aerodynamic styling of the 400 Superamerica and 500 Superfast with the 275 GTS: what Dean Batchelor once called "a combination that could have been a disaster." However, in the skilled hands of Pininfarina, the juxtaposition of design elements from two Berlinettas and a Spyder turned into an extraordinarily attractive coupe.

A truly modern Ferrari for the times, it featured four-wheel fully independent suspension with unequal-length A-arms, coil springs and telescopic shock absorbers, disc brakes on all four wheels, and a five-speed, all-synchromesh transmission built in-unit with the differential to deliver 300 horsepower from the Colombo-based V12.

The 330 GTC was closer than any model had yet come to combining the power of a Ferrari V12 with the unadulterated luxury of a touring car. It was fast, comfortable, and quiet. It even had air conditioning as an option.

Being all things to all people has always been a difficult task, but Ferrari made one remarkable overture to that end with the 330 GTC. Production lasted from mid-1966 to the end of 1968, at which time the engine was enlarged to 4.4 liters and the car renamed the 365 GTC. This version was continued through 1969.

As Ferrari prepared to enter the 1970s, an entirely new line of road and competition cars was under development—cars that would once again break new ground in design, performance, and engineering. Exactly two years after the 275 GTB/4 had appeared on the Ferrari stand in Paris, the all-new 365 GTB/4 Daytona made its debut, and from that moment on, all bets were off.

In 1972 a new sales arrangement was created for Ferrari North America. In the eastern United States, a partnership was formed by the Chinettis and Al Garthwaite. In the West, where the Von Newmann brothers at Competition Motors had handled sales, the new importer was Modern Classic Motors in Reno, Nevada, owned by the renowned car collector and casino owner Bill Harrah.

This was the arena that had been established by Chinetti, and as a new decade was dawning, the true heirs were about to set foot upon the stage. Ferrari would stun the motoring world with sports and racing cars unlike any that had yet come from Maranello.

Chapter 8

Nothing says Ferrari like red. Screaming out loud, hold on to the seat of your pants, drop dead red; and no Ferrari was better suited to that color than the 365 GTB/4 Daytona. This was the car that gave young men pause to reconsider their futures; a car upon which aspirations could be built.

The words *Berlinetta* and *Spyder* are two of the most important in the Ferrari language, words that define the essence of the automobile before one even knows the year or model. So it was to be with the 365 GTB/4, which for many Ferrari collectors has become the ultimate example of these differing approaches to design.

The Ferrari Daytona was introduced in Europe as a Berlinetta in 1968 and as a Spyder the following year. Displayed at the Paris Motor Show, the prototype coupe was actually the third Daytona design created by Carrozzeria Pininfarina but the first to use the new 365 motor and to resemble the production car closely. Built on a 275 GTB chassis, every body panel and piece of glass was different from the later 365 GTB/4 production models, and the 1968 prototype was the only Daytona actually built by Pininfarina. The production car bodies were built for Ferrari by Scaglietti.

Since Ferrari began offering road cars in the late 1940s, the Berlinetta design had evolved into one of Maranello's most popular body styles for both road and competition cars. Ferrari styling had for years dictated that every car have a dynamic grille, and a pronounced, aggressive visage, epitomized by models such as the 250 MM, 340 Mexico, Tour de France, and 250 GTO. For the Daytona, however, Sergio Pininfarina and his staff were about to take a detour, departing from all previous Ferrari models and abandoning for the first time the oval grille that had become a Ferrari hallmark.

Breaking from tradition was a difficult decision for Sergio Pininfarina. For more than a decade he had designed bodies for Ferrari that were imbued with a sense of heritage and, however different they may have been from model to model, always had a look that was unmistakably Ferrari. The 250 GTO, 250 GTB Lusso, and 275 GTB had been the first cars significantly to advance aerodynamic design at Ferrari, but they had still borne the traditional Ferrari styling cues. As he began designing a body for the new 365 GT engine and driveline, Pininfarina was convinced that aerodynamics were now as important as the car's performance. Thus he decided to replace the aggressive oval grille with a sharp, thin line from the front, with the radiator intake forming a horizontal slit beneath the nose. In one bold stroke he had changed the Ferrari's formidable open mouth into a malevolent grin.

This new approach to front end styling presented one unique challenge: where to place the headlights, which had

Left and opposite: The first of their kind, the 1968 Ferrari 365 GTB/4 Berlinetta and 1969 Ferrari 365 GTS/4 Spyder prototypes. Both cars featured the Perspex nose band with concealed headlights, a stunning design that was not permitted in the United States.

for more than twenty years been a part of the fender design. With the 365 GTB/4, however, there were no front fenders, at least not in a conventional sense. This brief impasse led to the second most dramatic styling change in Ferrari history—the elimination of faired-in headlamps.

For the 365 GTB/4, Pininfarina chose to set the headlamps back under clear rectangular covers, which blended in with the lines of the front deck. Small horizontal bumpers were set into either side of the radiator air intake, with small parking lights tucked in just above and small, round marker lights positioned on each side of the front fenders. At least one prototype incorporating these changes was built in the late summer and early fall of 1968. On the final version, the paired headlamps were set slightly back from the nose of the car, but the entire nose was now covered by a single band of transparent plastic. This nose band—a sheet of Perspex approximately 8 inches high—was then carried around the front corners to integrate parking and side marker light units, ending just short of the front wheel arches. Toward either end, where it covered the four headlights, this plastic band was left essentially clear (there were fine, white vertical lines on the inner surface). In the center, the inner surface of the Perspex was painted

The Daytona's original design called for headlights concealed behind a clear plastic cover. The dynamic new design, however, was not in accordance with U.S. federal headlight height requirements and had to be changed for export models. Ferrari found it necessary to design a second front end, which positioned iodine headlamps in a retractable housing that mimicked the Perspex nose when the lights were off and "popped" up (Corvette-style) when they were turned on. All models originally sold in the United States were so equipped.

black (still with fine white, vertical lines), except for the very center, left clear to display the rectangular Ferrari emblem attached to the body work underneath.

There was, however, much more to the 365 GTB/4 than its radical new headlight design. The hood was a highly complex series of curves and one of the most difficult pieces on the entire car. On both sides and approximately halfway back, there were two recessed air vents, located in a low-pressure area and serving as outlets for warm air passing through the combined water and oil radiator. Adding to the complexity of the hood, the trailing edge was curved to conform to the base of the windshield, with the gap between the hood and windshield varying from a mere fraction of an inch at the sides to several inches along the centerline of the hood. At the same time, the plane of the hood bent sharply upward along the rear edge, giving the effect

The prototype Daytona (below) had a different trunk design, which did not extend down into the rear apron between the taillights. The car was built on a 275 GTB chassis, and every body panel and piece of glass was different from the later 365 GTB/4 production models, and the 1968 prototype was the only Daytona actually built by Pininfarina.

of a louver and in theory directing the air flow up to the windshield rather than bluntly into it.

The large gap created by the curve of the hood as it rounded the windshield served a dual purpose: as an additional outlet for engine compartment air and as a storage space to park the windshield wipers. In theory, the wipers were supposed to be removed from the line of vision through the windshield, thereby precluding annoying reflections and, by tucking them behind the louver at the rear of the

hood, improving aerodynamics. In actual practice, the wipers had to be parked in view in order to clean the windshield.

A factory press release noted that the large, double-curved windshield had "an extremely aerodynamic line" and was sharply angled to the rear. It was attached to the body without a visible rubber gasket, which was recessed to improve the smoothness of the lines and covered by a thin strip of bright metal surrounding the windshield.

There was a decidedly rakish angle to the Daytona's roof line,

Ferrari and Pininfarina introduced the world to the all-new 365 GTB/4 Daytona at the Paris Motor Show in October 1968. At that time it was the most expensive (at just under $20,000) and fastest (the factory claim of 174 miles per hour was verified, within 1 mile per hour, in a 1970 *Road & Track* test) road car in the company's history. This is the actual prototype car as it appeared in 1968. The first factory sales brochure was printed in three languages: French, Italian, and English.

LA FERRARI COSTRUISCE IN PICCOLA SERIE MOTORI A 12
CILINDRI DAL 1946 E LE SUE VERE GRANTURISMO COM
PENDIANO LE ESPERIENZE DIRETTE DI 22 ANNI DI VIT
TORIOSE AFFERMAZIONI.

DEPUIS 1946 FERRARI CONSTRUIT EN PETITE SÉRIE DES
MOTEURS 12 CYLINDRES ET LES VOITURES ACTUELLES DE
GRAND TOURISME SONT LA PANACÉE DE 22 ANS D'EXPÉ
RIENCES VICTORIEUSES.

FERRARI HAVE BEEN MANUFACTURING LIMITED PRODU
CTION 12 CYLINDER ENGINES OF VARIOUS CAPACITY SIN
CE 1946 AND THEIR RANGE
OF THOROUGHBRED GRAN
TURISMO CARS INCORPORA
TES THE DIRECT EXPERIEN
CES OF 22 YEARS OF UNEQUAL
LED RACING SUCCESSES

365 GTB 4 *pininfarina*

Ferrari

365 GTB 4 *pininfarina*

The graceful lines of the 365 GTB/4 Daytona Berlinetta rewrote the book on Ferrari design. Both examples shown are the European models with the Perspex nose not approved for sale in the United States.

establishing a fastback appearance at the rear of the body before angling down to the deck lid and an extremely large and almost flat backlight. This was installed in a manner similar to that of the windshield and surrounded by a thin strip of brightwork. The tail section of the fastback was taken up with the rear-deck lid, which ended along the rear edge of the upper body work on the prototype but extended down between the paired round taillights on production versions.

With only a few exceptions—most notably the 1962 250 GT Lusso—Ferrari Berlinettas were notorious for restricted rear vision. The Daytona would not follow suit. In designing the 365 GTB/4, Pininfarina used taller side windows, extending upward from the belt line to the flat roof line, allowing drivers improved over-the-shoulder visibility. The door glass featured front vent windows on each side, and aft of the door glasses, in the rear sail panels, were rear quarter windows, followed in turn by a set of crescent-shaped air outlet vents, which were painted black. The entire window ensemble was surrounded by bright, thin metal frames and an additional piece of

brightwork along the drip molding above the windows to accent the roof line. Overall, the large expanses of glass helped lighten the visual effect of the rear half of the car as well as provide much improved driver visibility.

In keeping with Pininfarina's decision to eliminate unnecessary embellishments, the trim around the windows was just about the only evidence of brightwork or decoration. Even conventional door handles were eliminated. Instead, small levers swiveled out parallel to the bottom of the door windows, looking more like part of the window trim. On the rear center of each door there was a small key lock, and that was all Pininfarina allowed to impair the smooth flow of the body lines.

One of the most significant styling characteristics of the 365 GTB/4 was the troughline, a concave molding used to create a visual divide between the upper and lower body panels without resorting to the use of chrome trim. Encircling three-fourths of the car, it extended the length of the body from behind the front wheel arches to those at the rear and then around the back of the body above the bumpers. The troughline was derived from the indent along the top third of a long-blade knife or bayonet. The sides of the Daytona were also somewhat narrowed in appearance by the

sharp inward slant of the rocker panels, giving the car an almost barrel-sided roll between the wheel arches.

Filling the void left earlier in the year by the discontinued 275 GTB/4 Berlinetta, the all-new Daytona made an immediate splash when introduced at the Paris Motor Show; however, it was not immediately available, and Ferrari did not produce the cars in any great number until the last half of 1969. Although it was the first Ferrari to be built in quantity to meet the U.S. regulations, the European version was marketed first, and the U.S. legal cars were not available on a regular basis until mid-1970. Real quantities did not arrive until early 1972, when the new U.S. Ferrari importers took over.

The Daytona Berlinetta interiors were beautifully designed, luxurious, and for the late 1960s, as modern in appearance as the car itself.

On models sold in the United States, the 4.4-liter (268-cubic inch) sixty-degree, double-overhead cam V12 delivered 352 horsepower at 7,500 revolutions per minute.

In all probability the 365 GTB/4 shown in Paris was the final Pininfarina prototype finished in a bright Ferrari racing red, with a red and black interior. The prototype built on chassis 11795 stayed with the factory until it was sold to one of their Formula One drivers, Arturo Merzario, in December 1970, and is now in a private collection.

Ironically, the car's most attractive feature, the Perspex-covered headlights, became its greatest handicap when Ferrari went to sell the Daytona in the United States. The headlights were not in accordance with federal height requirements. Ferrari found it necessary to design a second front end just for export to the United States. The second design positioned iodine headlamps in a retractable housing

that mimicked the Perspex nose when the lights were off and "popped" up Corvette-style when they were turned on, at which point Pininfarina's aerodynamic theory of an unbroken front surface was spoiled.

The body of the new car was not the only innovation. In order to meet federal emissions regulations that went into effect in the United States in 1968, Ferrari's engineers had to come up with an efficient, clean-burning engine.

The 365 GTB/4 model's designation followed the Ferrari custom of stating the displacement of a single cylinder, followed by a set of letters and numerals that further defined the car. Thus, the new Berlinetta had 365 cubic centimeters per cylinder (precisely, 4,390.35 cubic centimeters total displacement), was a Gran Turismo Berlinetta, and had an engine with four camshafts.

Above: Coming or going, this was the look, and the model, Americans and Europeans came to regard as the ultimate Ferrari road car in the late 1960s.

By the late 1960s, Enzo Ferrari, shown in front of the Maranello factory main entrance, had established himself as the most prominent manufacturer of sports and racing cars in the world. The name Ferrari was recognized on every continent and in every language.

Although the Daytona Spyder was first shown in 1969, it was not available until 1971. The prototype car pictured (serial number 12851) was the only example built with the Perspex-covered European headlights. Any other Spyders with such covers were either retrofitted by the owner or converted from European Berlinettas to Spyders, a common practice in the 1980s.

The new sixty-degree, double-overhead-cam V12 was derived from earlier designs by Gioacchino Colombo and Aurelio Lampredi. Displacing 4.4 liters (268 cubic inches) and teamed with six Weber DCN20 twin-barrel 40-millimeter downdraft carburetors, the fed-legal Ferrari engine delivered 352 horsepower at 7,500 revolutions per minute, taking the drive through a ZF all-synchromesh five-speed transaxle built in-unit with the differential.

Following the 275 GTB/4, the Daytona had a four-wheel independent suspension composed of unequal-length A-arms with tubular shock absorbers, coil springs, and front and rear antiroll bars. The Daytonas were also equipped with Dunlop ventilated disc brakes on all four wheels.

Underneath, a welded tubular steel ladder frame supported the car's 94.5-inch wheelbase and wider than normal 56.6-inch front and rear track. The Berlinetta's broad stance was contrasted by an overall length of 174.2 inches (14.5 feet).

At the time of its introduction, the 365 GTB/4 Berlinetta was the most expensive and fastest road car in Ferrari's twenty-one-year history. Priced at just under $20,000, the Daytona was capable of reaching a top speed of 174 miles per hour according to the factory. *Road & Track* recorded zero to 60 in 5.9 seconds and a top speed of 173 mph.

Following the successful introduction of the Daytona Berlinetta, work was begun on a Spyder version, to be introduced in 1969. Although building Spyders was becoming something of a tradition around Ferrari, beheading the 365 GTB/4 flew in the face of reason. Designed to take advantage of Europe's high-speed autoroutes, the Daytona was the most aerodynamic model in Ferrari's history. Pininfarina claimed that the outline of the body had been developed, both in general lines and in many smaller details, in accordance with studies conducted in the wind tunnel at the Turin Polytechnic Institute. Aerodynamics was as much a part of the car's performance as the refined V12 engine under the hood. If the roof was removed, the aerodynamic gains were gone with the wind, so to speak. Making a Daytona Spyder was not logical. Of course, who said logic has anything to do with automobiles?

"In Europe, we are accustomed to thinking of a sports car as a Berlinetta. On the contrary, a sports car for an American many times means a Spyder," explains Sergio Pininfarina. In total, 1,383 Daytonas were produced, including 122 Spyders, 96 of which, not surprisingly, were sold to customers in the United States.

The interior of the Spyder was identical to that of the 365 GTB/4 Berlinetta, less, of course, a roof over your head and quarter windows.

Opposite: Mechanically, the 365 GTB/4 Berlinetta and Spyder were identical, although the Berlinetta showed consistently superior performance—the Spyder's reduced aerodynamics exacted their toll on top-end velocity. There were also a number of structural changes made to strengthen the convertible body, making the 365 GTS/4 heavier than the GTB/4. Heavier, too, was the price, a hefty $26,000 in 1973.

Ferrari got hooked on naming cars for the United States market when the company introduced the 340 America in 1951. It was followed in 1956 by the 410 Superamerica, and then the first Spyder California in December 1957.

The rarest cars to carry the California epithet were the 365 California Spyders, successors to the much-vaunted 500 Superfast models introduced in 1964. For Ferrari, these were to be uncommon cars, hand-built, high-performance luxury models. Even more exclusive in number than the Superfast, the 365 California would be limited to just ten months' production, from October 1966 to July 1967, allowing a mere thirteen cars, plus the Geneva prototype built in July 1966.

By name, the car was related to the legendary two-seat 250GT Spyder California, but by design, closer to the Superfast, with seating for four, albeit as a convertible rather than a coupe.

At the time the 365 California Spyder was penned, designer Sergio Pininfarina was planning to break away from traditional Ferrari styling with the all-new 365 GTB/4 Daytona. The 365 California Spyder fell somewhere in between past and future, a byproduct of Pininfarina's archetypal school of design and the company's emerging aerodynamic vogue.

The California Spyder represents an amazing composite of Ferrari designs, a 2+2 convertible uniting elements from the ritzy 500 Superfast, the luxurious 330 GTC, itself a compilation of designs, and the sleek 206 Dino, all seamlessly tied to the formidable power of Ferrari's new 4.4-liter, 320-horsepower V12. Like its luxury counterparts, the 365 offered power steering, power windows, and air conditioning.

While the California was nothing out of the ordinary under the skirts, basically a mirror image of the 330 GT 2+2, it was the only Ferrari convertible model at that time designed to seat four. Combined with Pininfarina's extraordinary body design, featuring pop-up driving lights, Dino-like door-into-fender air scoops, and uncharacteristically large, canted taillights, the 365 California Spyder was a unique car, even among Ferraris.

The example shown, serial Number 10077, was among the last four built in the series and has been a part of the renowned Nethercutt Collection in Sylmar, California, since 1981. It is one of the few contemporary automobiles deemed significant enough to share a place among the great American and European classics in the collection.

The interior featured the lavish use of polished wood veneers and hand-sewn leather upholstery throughout to make the 365 GT California Spyder one of the most luxurious Ferrari models of the 1960s.

The 365 GT California Spyder was an amazing composite of Ferrari designs: a 2+2 convertible uniting elements from the ritzy 500 Superfast, the luxurious 330 GTC, itself a compilation of designs, and the sleek 206 Dino. Combined with Pininfarina's extraordinary body design, featuring pop-up driving lights, Dino-like door-into-fender air scoops, and uncharacteristically large, canted taillights, the 365 California Spyder was the only four-seat Ferrari convertible model of the 1960s.

The F40 was one of those cars that beckoned you, no, compelled you,
if you had any spirit at all, to take hold of the wheel and master the machine.
It was how a seasoned horseman might have felt when he came upon a wild stallion.

Racing has been the foundation for nearly all of Ferrari's achievements in the design of road cars. One of the most significant was the development of the boxer engine in 1964. Ferrari's first flat, opposed (180-degree V12) boxer engine was a twelve-cylinder, 1.5-liter Formula One engine with 11:1 compression ratio, Lucas fuel injection, and output of 210 horsepower at a screaming 11,000 revolutions per minute.

The boxer name itself was derived from the pistons' reciprocating movement, back and forth, toward and away from each other, like two boxers sparring. The term, however, was actually of German origin, used to describe the layout of the early Porsche and VW four-cylinder engines, which were also of flat-opposed design.

The 365 GT4 Berlinetta Boxer—Ferrari's first mid-engine production sports car (discounting the Fiat-powered Dino)—was fitted with a 4.4-liter production version of the competition engine in 1974. Mounted behind the driver and ahead of the rear axle, it delivered 380 horsepower at 7,200 revolutions per minute.

The 365 GT4 BB would be the first of a generation of new rear-engine twelve-cylinder models, which would remain in production for more than twenty years. The main body structure of the 365 GT4 was steel, with the hood, doors, and rear-deck lid made of aluminum and the lower body panels constructed of fiberglass. As usual, the design was by Pininfarina with the actual body production handled by Carrozzeria Scaglietti in Modena.

The styling of the 512 Berlinetta Boxer was already established with the 365 GT4 BB, but updated by Carrozzeria Pininfarina with the addition of a spoiler under the grille, which squared up the front end perspective, and NASA ducts on the lower body sides forward of the wheel openings.

"A Ferrari should be designed to always show the engine, because that is the heart of the machine," says Sergio Pininfarina. This dictum was never more apparent than in the sculptured engine cover of the 512 BB, a stylistic work of art that focused attention on the Ferrari engine as never before. Beneath the deck lid was an equally attractive engine, the Forghieri-based flat-opposed V12 designed to look as impressive as it felt under full throttle.

The most famous taillights in Ferrari's sixty-year history, the twin round lenses of the 512 BB model. This design would be repeated on numerous Ferrari models.

The 365 GT4 BB (Boxer) and 512 BB were fairly large cars, built on a wheelbase measuring 2,500 millimeters (98.4 inches), almost 4 inches longer than the 275 GTB/4 and 365 GTB/4 models preceding them. The cars' overall length was accentuated by the long front overhang and the height of the rear deck.

The cars utilized the latest Ferrari suspension technology, with unequal-length A-arms, coil springs, tubular shock absorbers, and antiroll bars front and rear. Dean Batchelor noted in his review of the 365 GT4 BB, "Handling is great for the enthusiast driver. The steering, which is heavy at low speeds, lightens up as speed increases and the tail-heavy weight distribution (43/57 percent), which would normally cause oversteer, is offset by a suspension with understeer designed into it—resulting in an agile, maneuverable car."

The 365 GT4 BB was the first Ferrari road car in many years to give drivers a taste of what a race car actually felt like. Ferrari produced the car until late in 1976, when the 512 Berlinetta Boxer took its place. The body styling of the 512 was almost identical to that of its predecessor. Pininfarina's revised styling added a chin spoiler (air dam) beneath the egg-crate front grille and air ducts on the lower body sides forward of the rear wheels. Other changes included the now famous 512 BB taillight array, with two large, round lenses per side, reprised on the 1995 Ferrari F 512 M.

The 512 BB employed the same blended media construction as the 365 GT4 BB, using steel for the main body structure; aluminum for the hood, doors, and engine cover; and glass fiber for the lower body panels. The use of glass fiber led to the most distinctive and memorable styling characteristic of both the 365 and the 512: a solid division line between the upper and lower body panels. On the 365, the lower part was always painted matte black. The two-tone color scheme was also available as an option on the 512 BB.

Displacement of the Forghieri-based 180-degree V12 engine used in the 512 BB was enlarged to 4,942 cubic centimeters (up from

Opposite:
The use of glass fiber led to the most distinctive styling feature of the 365 and the 512: a solid division line between the upper and lower body panels. On the 365, the lower part was always painted matte black, whereas the two-tone color scheme was optional on the 512 BB.

The 512 BBi (1981–84) rang down the curtain on what was, for the time, the most powerful road car ever put into the hands of everyday drivers. The BBi utilized Bosch K-Jetronic fuel injection, replacing the four 40IF3C carburetors used on the 512 BB. Output remained unchanged, but 340 horsepower now arrived at 6,000 revolutions per minute rather than 6,800 rpm.

4,390 in the 365) by a bore increase of 1 millimeter to 87-millimeters and an increase in the stroke of 7 millimeters to 78 millimeters. While output from the revised boxer engine was actually decreased by 5.2 percent (down from 380 horsepower to 360 horsepower), peak horsepower was reached at 6,200 revolutions per minute instead of 7,200, an interesting trade-off.

Both the 365 and 512 boxers were raced by private entrants, but their time in the sun was brief and the racing effort short-lived. They were by far, however, the best road cars Ferrari had brought to market up to that time. Dean Batchelor wrote of the 512 BB, "The boxers are fantastic cars to drive, with little raison d'être other than the sheer pleasure of driving the ultimate sporting GT car." Almost

The longest-running model in Ferrari history, the 308 was produced from 1974 through the 1980s and with continuing improvements culminating with the 308GTBi and 308GTB Qv (Quattrovalve) models.

thirty years after its introduction, the 512 BB, with its razor-edge styling and incomparable mid-engine layout, remains one of the most desirable Ferraris, a car that still looks like it is going 200 miles per hour while standing still.

Evolution in design has led to many of Ferrari's most outstanding and best loved road cars, but none became more ubiquitous than the 308 GTB and GTS, probably the most recognized Ferrari ever produced, thanks in part to the television series *Magnum, P.I.*, starring Tom Selleck. Moreover, Ferrari enthusiasts, who flocked to dealer-

ships for the lowest-priced model in years, found this to be the most practical driver's car in Ferrari history.

Pininfarina stylists combined the best attributes of the 246 Dino and 365 GT Berlinetta Boxer in the 308's design. Suspension was all independent in the then traditional Ferrari layout, and the car was powered by a four-cam, ninety-degree V8 engine mounted transversely, just ahead of the rear axle. The 308 offered a spirited 255 horsepower at 7,700 revolutions per minute, and drove through a five-speed transmission. An open version of the

Far left:
One of Ferrari's longest-lived road cars was a true *boulevardier*. The 400 GT was introduced in 1976 and succeeded by the 400i GT in 1979 and the 412 in 1985. These were the first full-size 2+2 luxury touring cars to be equipped with automatic transmission.

The 400i was the most luxurious Ferrari of its time, and the first to compete in the luxury touring car market against Mercedes-Benz, BMW, and Maserati. The car could be equipped with either a GM automatic or a five-speed gearbox. The interior of the 400i was completely redesigned from that of the 1976–79 400 2+2. Available as an option was dual (front and rear) air conditioning.

308, with a removable roof section similar to that used on the 246 Dino and the Porsche 911 Targa, was added to the line in 1977.

The longest running model in Ferrari history, the 308 continued on into the 1980s in improved versions, the 308GTBi, 308GTB Qv (Quattrovalve), and 328 Berlinetta and Spyder.

Another of Ferrari's longest-lived road cars was a true *boulevardier*, the 400 GT, introduced in 1976 and succeeded by the 400i GT in 1979 and the 412 in 1985. These were the first full-size 2+2 luxury Ferrari touring cars to be equipped with an automatic transmission. Unfortunately, the initial models were not imported into the United States because of specific safety standards and EPA emissions certification issues.

Beginning in 1982, two years after Ferrari North America replaced Chinetti-Garthwaite Imports and Modern Classics as the sole U.S. importer, the decision was made to allow the European specification 400i to be sold through American Ferrari dealerships for customer delivery at the factory in Maranello. Once driven in Italy by the owner, the car could be shipped to the United States under a provision allowing an individual to import a "used" car from Europe or abroad.

At this point in time, European specification models from Ferrari, Lamborghini, Mercedes-Benz, and other foreign automakers were also being brought into the United States as gray-market cars, modified and emissions certified by independent firms, which in turn sold

Luxurious, yes, but still a Ferrari, the 400i was powered by a 4,823-cubic-centimeter sixty-degree V12 with an output of 310-horsepower at 6,400 revolutions per minute, later increased to 315 at 6,400 rpm after September 1982.

the cars. They were not, however, under warranty through U.S. distributorships. The decision to offer factory deliveries gave U.S. Ferrari dealers parity with the independent importers and took at least one European-only model off the market. In addition, it gave owners the full factory warranty and a car that could be serviced at any Ferrari dealership in the country.

As a whole, the era of gray-market imports in the 1980s was not one of the automotive industry's finer moments; some of the European models were not acceptably modified for U.S. roads, nor were

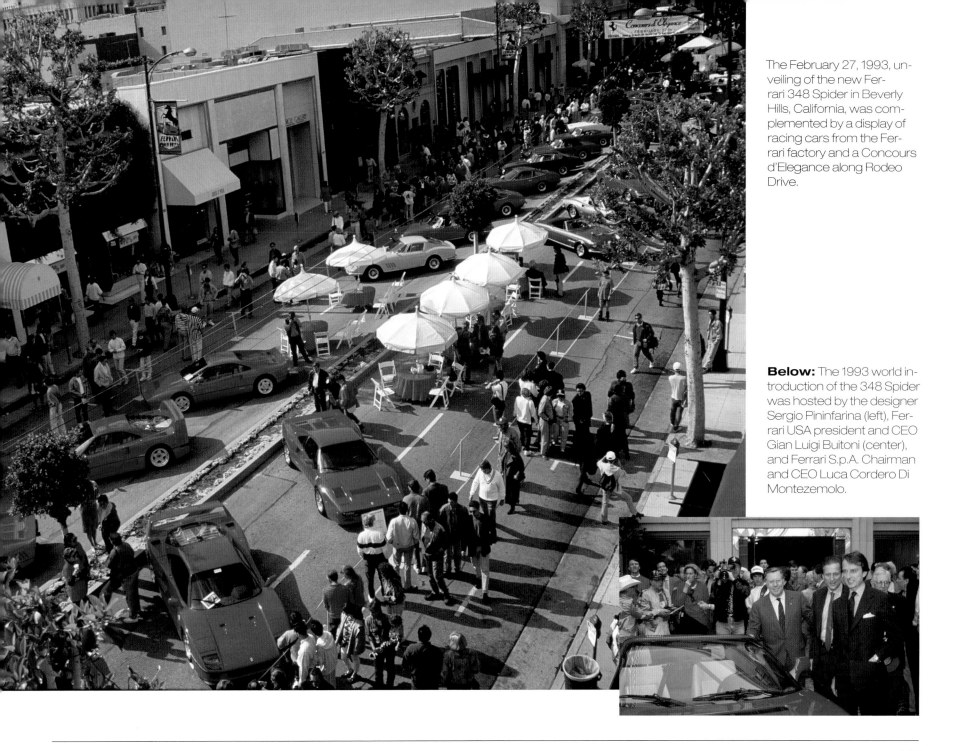

The February 27, 1993, unveiling of the new Ferrari 348 Spider in Beverly Hills, California, was complemented by a display of racing cars from the Ferrari factory and a Concours d'Elegance along Rodeo Drive.

Below: The 1993 world introduction of the 348 Spider was hosted by the designer Sergio Pininfarina (left), Ferrari USA president and CEO Gian Luigi Buitoni (center), and Ferrari S.p.A. Chairman and CEO Luca Cordero Di Montezemolo.

The 348 was the first two-seat convertible since the 365 GTB/4 Daytona Spyder, last sold in 1974, and also the first mid-engine two-seat Ferrari Spider ever. (Note that Ferrari had changed the spelling of Spyder, with a *y* when referring to the Daytona, to an *i* when addressing later models.) The Spider was the evolution of the 348 tb/ts series announced in 1989. Power for the mid-engine 348 convertible was Ferrari's proven ninety-degree light-alloy V8.

The Ferrari Challenge Series put the 348 (shown in the *Speciale* Berlinetta edition) and later F 355 models into competition with driver-owners who have qualified under Sports Car Club of America standards. The series promoted owner enthusiasm for and appreciation of Ferrari's proud racing heritage. It also gave owners a chance to find out what a Ferrari was capable of under actual race conditions.

their emissions up to EPA standards. As a result, a number of importers were fined, others shut down, and, in some instances, the cars seized and impounded.

The 400i was the most luxurious Ferrari of its time and the first to compete in the luxury touring car market against Mercedes-Benz, BMW, and Maserati's 4-Port. The cars could be equipped with either a GM automatic or a five-speed gearbox. The interior of the 400i was completely redesigned from that of the 1976–79 400 2+2. Also available as an option was dual, front, and rear air conditioning. It was luxurious but still a

Ferrari. The 400i was powered by a 4,823-cubic-centimeter sixty-degree V12 with an output of 310 horsepower at 6,400 revolutions per minute, increased to 315 at 6,400 RPM after September 1982.

The 1995 Ferrari 456 GT 2+2 took up where the 400i and 412 had left off a decade earlier, presenting owners with a luxurious four-passenger touring car built in the Ferrari tradition. The car featured a clean-sheet-of-paper 442-horsepower V12, six-speed transmission, and electronically actuated, fully independent suspension, as well as state-of-the-art traction control and antilock braking.

288 GTO

Another *Gran Turismo Omologato*

In 1985 Ferrari resurrected the *Gran Turismo Omologato* acronym GTO and attached it to a new 308-derived sports racing model. With a more distinctive front end and additional ducting at the rear, the 288 GTO concealed a mid-mounted, twin-turbocharged V8 engine.

The car had been introduced a year before in March at the annual Geneva show, and although appearing to be a street car, it was in fact a Group B homologated GT racer. For a model to be homologated, Ferrari had to produce two hundred cars, and, unlike with the first example to bear the GTO name, Maranello not only built but quickly sold all two hundred 288 GTOs by word of mouth alone! The demand became so high, in fact, that fabricators in the United States began converting 308 models into 288 GTO copies.

Sales of the factory cars were allocated by country, with the United States receiving sixty. The balance was divided among Italy, which retained forty-five examples; Germany, receiving only twenty-one; France, fifteen; Switzerland, fourteen; Great Britain, thirteen; Belgium, seven; and the balance of twenty-five for the rest of the world.

With the Twin IHI turbocharged Ferrari V8 mounted longitudinally, rather than transversely, as on the 308 and 328, the rear wheels had to be moved back 110 millimeters (a little more than 4 inches), and rear luggage space was sacrificed as well.

A Group B homologated GT racer, Ferrari had to produce two hundred cars for homologation, but unlike the first GTO Maranello not only built but quickly sold all two hundred 288 GTOs by word of mouth alone! The engine was accompanied by twin IHI turbochargers and was mounted longitudinally, rather than transversely, as on the 308 and 328.

The 288 GTO engine was formulated on the 308GTB Qv (Quattrovalve) block but the bore was *reduced* to 80 millimeters in order to lower the engine's swept volume to 2,855 cubic centimeters. This became necessary because of the Japanese-built IHI turbochargers and homologation rules requiring no more than a 1.4 times equivalence ratio among supercharged, turbocharged, and normally aspirated engines. Therefore, the maximum allowable capacity to homologate a turbocharged engine was 2,857 cubic centimeters, a mere 2 cubic centimeters more than that of the 288 GTO's engine! Output was rated at no less than 400 horsepower with the twin turbos engaged. Top speed was around 190 miles per hour.

Almost every Ferrari sports racing model was a success, but the 288 GTO has a postscript. After the first two hundred were built, demand was still so high that another seventy-one cars were assembled in 1985.

After the 512 BB (1976–81) and 512 BBi (1981–84) concluded production, the flat-opposed twelve-cylinder design found a new home in a stunningly innovative, all-new model that would resurrect a historic name from Ferrari's past, Testa Rossa.

In the fall of 1984, Ferrari unveiled the Testarossa (now one word) in Modena on the site of the original Scuderia Ferrari facility in the heart of town. The name Testarossa, meaning "red head," had been taken from one of Ferrari's most legendary race cars, the 250 Testa Rossa, which had rampaged across Europe in the late 1950s. And, like its namesake, the 1985 Testarossa was a radical departure from conventional Ferrari design. Pininfarina had pulled out all the stops, taking form and function to a new level by essentially designing the body around the engine, a 4,942-cubic-centimeter flat twelve delivering

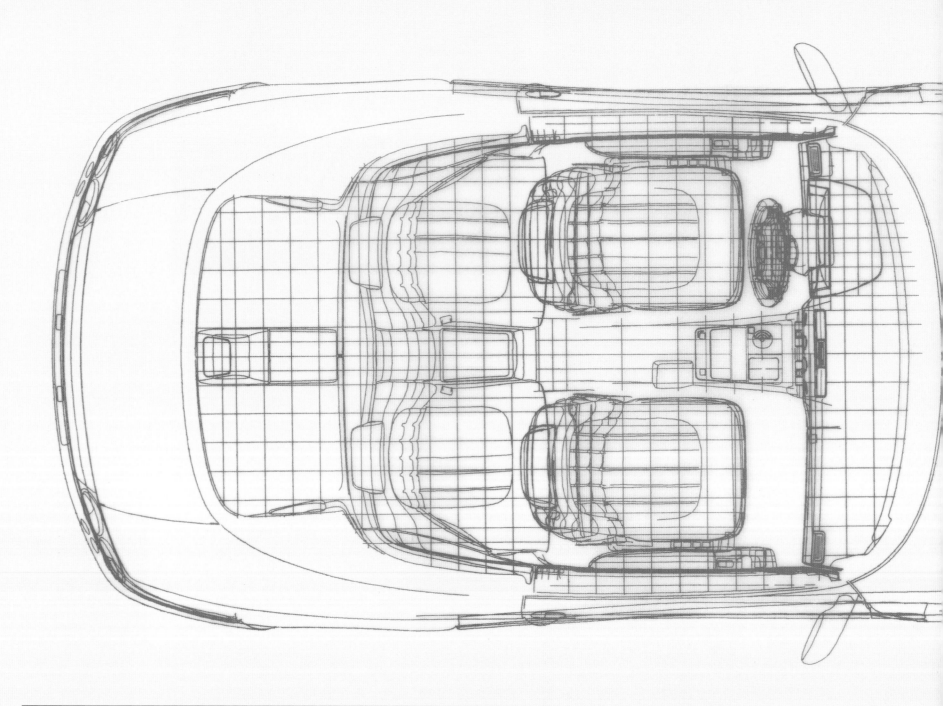

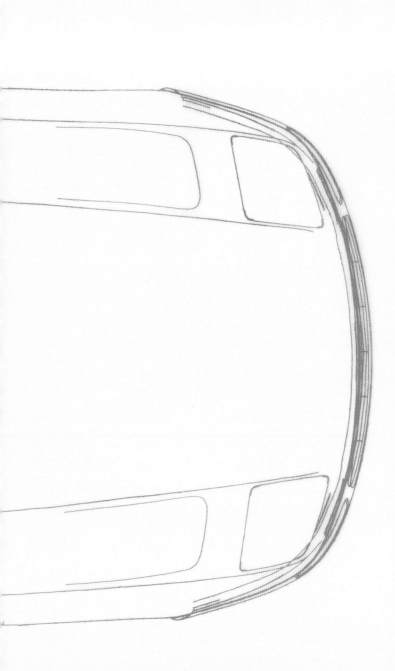

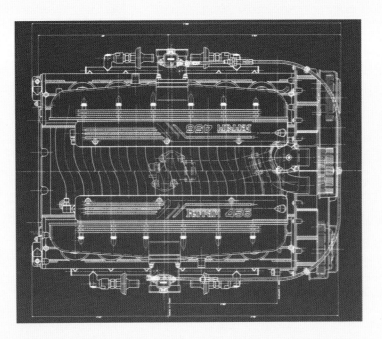

390 horsepower at 6,300 revolutions per minute in European trim and 380 horsepower in U.S. specification.

The most outstanding aspect of the design was the horizontal air intake strakes rending their way through the doors and into the rear fenders. This became the car's most distinctive characteristic, and one that has never been successfully duplicated, except by Ferrari in the Testarossa's two succeeding models, the 512 TR and the F 512 M.

Back in 1987, when Ferrari celebrated its fortieth anniversary, Modena introduced the F40. The name was chosen to commemorate the production of Ferrari automobiles from 1947 to 1987, but the F40 was no badge-engineered commemorative issue. It was the

first Ferrari since the 512 BB that was closer to a race car than a road car. It was also the least practical Ferrari ever produced, although, in the spirit of the original sports cars built in Modena forty years earlier, the F40 was the ideal model to honor Ferrari's anniversary year. It was a sports car pure and simple.

The body was a Kevlar and carbon composite shell surrounding a tubular steel, Kevlar, and carbon composite framework, to which Ferrari had mounted a 478-horsepower, twin-turbocharged dual-overhead-camshaft, four-valve V8 engine and a highly articulated four-wheel independent suspension. Little more was needed to take an F40 into competition than some additional safety equipment and numbers on the doors.

A recessed latch opened the lightweight doors, allowing the driver to climb or drop, depending upon style or build, into the contoured racing seat. Getting out of or into the F40 became a learned art, like that of the 300 SL Gullwing. Until drivers mastered ingress and egress, they were disposed to bruising hips and shoulders along with several other vital parts of the human anatomy that become subject to impact if one slides into the cockpit the wrong way.

For the $250,000 originally asked by the factory (prices approached $1 million as speculators bought and resold cars throughout the late 1980s), one received a great deal of sensory gratification with the F40, but little else. The interior had a full complement of

The second coming of the Testarossa became one of Ferrari's most successful road cars, with production lasting from 1985 to 1996. From the first Testarossa models built (pictured) through 512 TR and F 512 M, this body style remained unsurpassed as the benchmark design of the 1980s.

The fortieth-anniversary Ferrari, better known as the F40, became one of the most speculative models in Ferrari history. At a suggested retail price of $250,000, the limited-edition cars soared to nearly $1 million as speculators and investors traded them around like commodities until the sports car market crashed in the early 1990s. The bold, mid-engine F40 was a pure, brute force street car that, with the addition of a roll cage and fire extinguisher, was ready to race.

The two views most other drivers saw of the F40, one in their rear view mirror, the other through the windshield. The cars were easily capable of 185 miles per hour.

gauges, everything the driver needed to know, and nothing more. No twelve-way power adjustable seats with driver memory. No power windows or accessories. Virtually no interior trim, not even door panels or door handles; you just pulled the cable slung in the hollow of the door and it unlatched. And no radio. Had there been one, it would have required a 300-watt system to boost the volume over the engine, because the F40 had virtually no interior soundproofing.

Even if it had, who needed music? The deep bass exhaust note under throttle, the treble whine of the V8, and the rhythm of the Pirelli P Zeros beneath you were a symphony for the senses.

The F40 was all pretty simple. You stepped on the gas pedal, the car went fast, very fast; you hit the brakes, it stopped; you turned the wheel, and it went where you pointed. Just the way Enzo Ferrari intended things to be.

Ferrari and Pininfarina paid little attention to the interior of the F40 other than to make it functional. Soundproofing was at a minimum, the dashboard was carpeted, and there were no accessories. Even the door panels were hollow. The angled cord in the recess was used to unlatch the door from inside, and the door glass was raised and lowered with old fashioned hand cranks.

The F40 was the closest Ferrari came to building a pure race car for the street.

The F 512 M was a glorious revival of the 1991 512 TR, itself a generation beyond the first Ferrari Testarossa. The F 512 M drew upon history as well for its name, resurrected from the 512 Berlinetta Boxer. This car also had another historical imperative. It was to be the first "interim" Ferrari model in decades.

An improved version of the Testarossa, re-styled by Pininfarina hard on the heels of the new F355 Berlinetta and the 456 GT 2+2 in 1995, the F 512 M was destined to be discontinued, and everyone knew it. This was a car that would be judged as few had. Not by the press, whose opinions are often taken too seriously, but by the very owners who would plunk down hard-earned lire for a car whose fate had already been sealed. The F 512 M was to be the end of the line for the boxer engine, a line that concluded an eleven-year run in 1996, when the F 512 M was officially replaced by the 1997 550 Maranello, the first front-engine Berlinetta since the 365 GTB/4 Daytona.

Without overdoing the technical analysis, one could say very little of the original TR remained. Mechanically, the F 512 M was a generation beyond. The Formula One–inspired boxer design delivering a heart-pounding 440 horsepower at 6,750 revolutions per minute, a full 50 horsepower better than the old Testarossa and 12 more than the 512TR. With 367 pounds/feet of torque at 5,500 rpm, the new F 512 M had no difficulty vanquishing either of its predecessors. Zero to 60 was a scant 4.6 seconds, and top speed just 4 miles per hour short of 200!

From the exterior, the most striking visual change in the Pininfarina styling was the aggressive front, reminiscent of the F40 and tempered with a touch of the new 456 GT's graceful form in and around the grille.

The F 512 M was a lighter, more powerful, more agile, and better built version of the Testarossa, still as impressive in appearance as the original, generously wide on the exterior and incomprehensibly narrow

Pininfarina's penchant for displaying the Ferrari engine reached an all-time high with the F40's clear plastic engine cover, which gave everyone a look at the inner workings of this incredible sports car.

inside, a Coke bottle mounted on aluminum caps and propelled by a V12 that could snatch your breath away at full song, and leave you wishing for legendary roads to challenge. Indeed, the F 512 M was an interesting way to bid farewell to both the Testarossa and the venerable boxer engine.

Traditionally, Ferrari's new model introductions were held in Italy and throughout Europe before the cars were shown in the United States. However, no automobile, let alone a Ferrari, has ever been introduced to the world on a *city street*. Of course, Ferrari is no ordinary automobile, and Rodeo Drive in Beverly Hills, California, no ordinary street.

On Saturday, February 27, 1993, the most famous stretch of pavement west of Wall Street was closed to traffic and lined from one end to the other (some three city blocks) with more than 125

The F 355, introduced in 1994, improved upon the virtues of every Ferrari built over the previous half century. It was the first of the New Guard, the bold, the complete, the Ferrari for a generation of prancing horse devotees who had little in common with the wonderfully brutish cars of the past.

Ferraris, dating from 1948 to 1993. It was without question one of the most impressive displays of Ferraris ever assembled, and all for the introduction of the latest model, the 348 Spider.

The public debut of the new Ferrari was conducted by the designer Sergio Pininfarina and then Ferrari S.p.A. Chairman and CEO Luca Cordero Di Montezemolo, who told the crowd that Ferrari chose Beverly Hills and Rodeo Drive for the car's world introduction because California is very important to Ferrari.

Pininfarina said that creating a new design is not an easy task. "The fundamental problem that exists with any new design is always the same. Our cars have been the best or among the best in the world, the highest prestige for fifty years. Every new car then is a challenge, because each time we have to reaffirm that we are good enough to redesign a car which brings such satisfaction to the owner."

The F 355, in either Berlinetta or Spider (shown), was at the time the most powerful Ferrari ever produced with a naturally aspirated V8 engine. Output from the ninety-degree, 3.5-liter, forty-valve, dual-overhead-cam V8 was rated at 375 horsepower at 8,250 revolutions per minute. This exhilarating performance was tempered by a computer-controlled, fully independent suspension, antilock disc brakes, and variable ratio power steering.

The 348 was the first two-seat convertible since the 365 GTB/4 Daytona Spyder, last sold in 1974, and also the first mid-engine two-seat Ferrari Spider ever. (Note that Ferrari had changed the spelling of Spyder, with a *y* when referring to the Daytona, to an *i* when addressing the new model.)

The Spider was the evolution of the 348 tb/ts series announced in 1989. Power for the mid-engine 348 convertible was Ferrari's proven ninety-degree light-alloy V8. Displacing 3,405 cubic centimeters with an 85- x 75-millimeter bore and stroke, the four-valve-per-cylinder engine had an output rated at 312 horsepower at 7,200 revolutions per minute, and 228.6 pounds/foot of torque at 4,000 rpm. The transmission was a transverse five-speed gearbox.

Since the debut of the 348 Spider, Ferrari has introduced a new model almost every year, keeping a promise Di Montezemolo made in 1993. He summarized Ferrari's new, more aggressive design and marketing approach rather poignantly: "Ferrari's strongest asset is its technology. We have to show our ability to create new designs and to improve that technology. If you stop in our job, you lose." Ferrari has never lost.

Introduced in 1996, the F 355 Spider was the most elegant open Ferrari in history and only the second model in Ferrari lineage (the other was the 348) with a mid-engine configuration. In Ferrari's own words, the F 355 was the "combination of the tried and tested with the highly innovative." Those same words would have suited the first road cars offered by Ferrari, those bodied by Vignale, Touring, and Pinin Farina, cars that lent luxury to the Ferrari name for the first time.

The F355, introduced in 1994, improved on the virtues of every Ferrari built over the last half century. It was the first of a new era, the bold, the complete, the Ferrari for a generation of prancing horse devotees who have little in common with the wonderfully brutish cars of the past.

The F355, in either Berlinetta or Spider (1996), and the F355 F1 (1997) were the most powerful Ferrari models produced up to that time with a naturally aspirated V8 engine. Output from the ninety-degree, 3.5-liter, forty-valve, dual-overhead-camshaft V8 was 375 horsepower at 8,250 revolutions per minute. The car's exhilarating performance was tempered by sophisticated computer-controlled, fully independent suspension, antilock disc brakes, and variable ratio power steering.

The F355 became a sports car for those who sought the élan of the Cavallino Rampante but fell back in apprehension when thinking of a Ferrari as a daily driver. No more. The F355 brought Ferrari owners the same equanimity Porsche Carrera drivers had enjoyed for years. This was also the first Ferrari in history to feature an electronically operated convertible top.

In Ferrari's own words, the F355 was the "combination of the tried and tested with the highly innovative." Half a century before, this remark would have suited the first road cars offered by

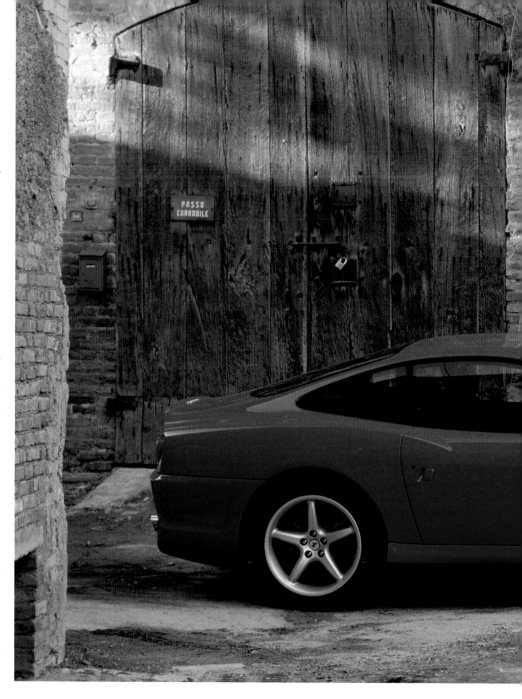

The 1997 model 550 Maranello replaced the F 512 M as Ferrari's performance flagship. The new SWB Berlinetta was the first front-engine V12 since the 365 GTB/4 Daytona. The 550 was powered by a version of the sixty-five-degree V12 used in the 456 GT. The car also shared the 456's driveshaft, light-alloy oil sump, and 334-cubic-inch displacement. The 48-valve, dual-overhead-camshaft V12 delivered 485 horsepower at 7,000 revolutions per minute through a six-speed manual transmission. Built on a 98.4-inch wheelbase chassis, the 550 was equipped with the same independent front and rear suspension and computer-controlled damping as used on the 1997 anniversary model F50.

Ferrari, those bodied by Vignale, Touring, and Pinin Farina, cars that lent luxury to the Ferrari name for the first time. The first Ferrari was an open-bodied car. The F355 Spider was the furthest stretch of the envelope at the time.

The future of Ferrari has taken the form of the most spectacular cars ever to come down the road from Maranello, models such as the 550 Barchetta, the Enzo, and 575M Maranello, and now the very latest Ferraris for the twenty-first century, the Superamerica, 612 Scaglietti, and F430 Berlinetta and Spider. Cars very different from their ancestors, yet each a Ferrari in its design and engineering, a sports car that can proudly wear the Cavallino Rampante and give each owner the same thrill when the engine ignites as Enzo Ferrari and Luigi Chinetti felt in 1947.

The Amazing F50
Cinquanta Anni

The F50 was the accumulation of forty-five racing models and endless Gran Turismo and Sports models. In theory, under the exotic Pininfarina-designed body, Ferrari's F50 was a road-going adaptation of the 1990 Ferrari 641/2 Formula One car.

Built around a central monocoque, and made entirely of Cytec Aerospace carbon fiber, the F50 had a total chassis weight of just 225 pounds. This formed the central part of the car, where the driver sits. Following Formula One design disciplines, the engine-gearbox-differential assembly was attached to the chassis with the engine anchoring the suspension, rear bumper, and body work elements. This was the first occasion that a system employing the engine as a structural element as well as the propulsion medium, had been used on a street vehicle.

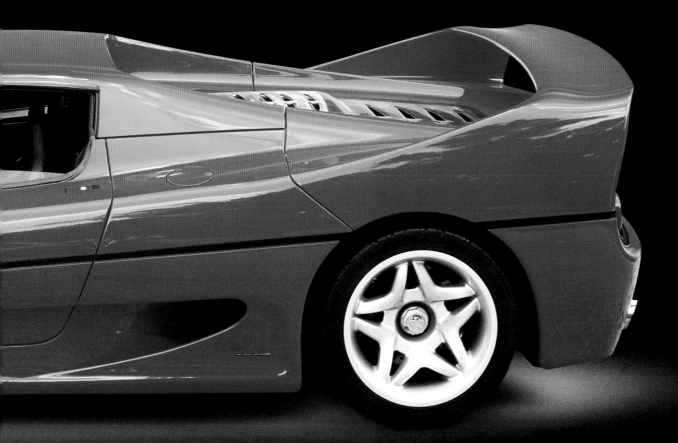

The F50's design placed 43 percent of the car's weight on the front axles and 57 percent over the rear. To guarantee a tendency to understeer, the front track measured 18 mm wider than the rear: 1,620 versus 1,602 mm.

Under 4,500 revolutions per minute, engine noise was muted. When you got into the power over 4,500 revs, the F50 trumpeted like a John Williams movie score. The engine actually changed temperament above 4,500 rpm, and the two-stage induction system opened fully to double the volume of air being delivered. At the same time, the Motronic control unit reduced back pressure on the exhaust. With the low-profile Fioranos it could paste you into the seatback in a heartbeat. Zero to 60 miles per hour time was 3.7 seconds. Less time than it takes to say it!

The styling of Ferrari's fiftieth anniversary model, the F50, was the most futuristic in the company's history until the 2002 Enzo. The body design by Pininfarina was a road car adaptation of Ferrari's Formula One race cars. The body was built entirely of composite material with carbon fiber, Kevlar by Cytec Aerospace, and Nomex honeycomb, in an aerodynamic curve that visually and functionally rose from the integrated front bumper to the profile of the rear wing.

There was an unusually solid sound when the doors closed, not the hollow thump you heard in the F40. The doors were upholstered and finely detailed. By comparison, the interior of the F50 was like that of a Rolls-Royce, and considerably more spacious than the F40's. Still, it was purely functional, the lower dash panel and most of the exposed interior surfaces made of carbon fiber. The floor mats were rubber. It was simple, but it had character.

Racing-style seats using a composite frame were luxuriously upholstered in Connolly leather surrounding red fabric inserts for the seatback and cushion. The driver's seat and pedal rack were both adjustable to tailor the car to each owner. Unlike the F40, a straightforward, no-frills road car with a race car temperament, the F50 was a bespoke Italian suit.

The most prominent feature of the clean, uncluttered interior layout was the center tunnel and shifter. The F50 gearbox was a wonderful blend of old and new. The high-tech carbon fiber shift knob and lever rested inches above a traditional polished steel shift gate, linking the driver to a six-speed transmission with ZF twin cone synchronizers and a limited slip differential.

Such technology must come in an appropriate package, and Carrozzeria Pininfarina pushed the envelope with the F50's styling. This was an outrageous-looking automobile, second only to the current Enzo model for pure audacity. With the massive air ducts in the hood, wide oval grille, and integrated headlights, when seen head on, the F50 almost appeared to be grinning. At nearly half a million dollars a copy when new, and with every one of the 349 cars built through 1997 having been pre-sold, someone in Maranello certainly was.

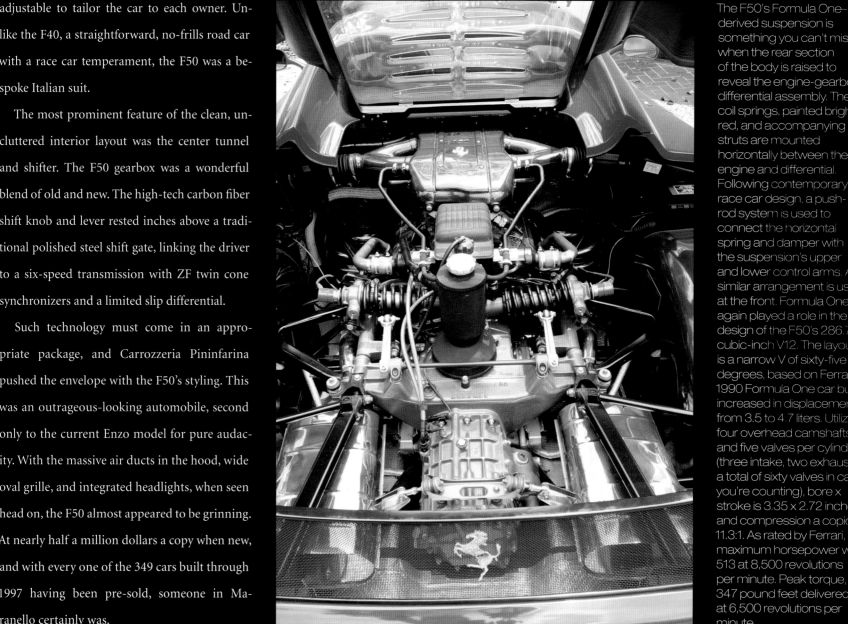

The F50's Formula One–derived suspension is something you can't miss when the rear section of the body is raised to reveal the engine-gearbox-differential assembly. The coil springs, painted bright red, and accompanying struts are mounted horizontally between the engine and differential. Following contemporary race car design, a push-rod system is used to connect the horizontal spring and damper with the suspension's upper and lower control arms. A similar arrangement is used at the front. Formula One again played a role in the design of the F50's 286.7-cubic-inch V12. The layout is a narrow V of sixty-five degrees, based on Ferrari's 1990 Formula One car but increased in displacement from 3.5 to 4.7 liters. Utilizing four overhead camshafts and five valves per cylinder (three intake, two exhaust—a total of sixty valves in case you're counting), bore x stroke is 3.35 x 2.72 inches and compression a copious 11.3:1. As rated by Ferrari, maximum horsepower was 513 at 8,500 revolutions per minute. Peak torque, 347 pound feet delivered at 6,500 revolutions per minute.

In 1999 and 2000, Ferrari introduced the 360 Modena and 360 Spider, respectively, the latter being the company's twentieth road-going convertible. Despite Ferrari's mid-mounted, 400-horsepower engine, stylists found a way to design a roof that automatically folded into its own well between the cabin and engine bay, thus creating a clean, uninterrupted line for the Spider, while preserving the classic Berlinetta back-light in the 360 Modena.

Perhaps the ultimate expression of racing-inspired design, the 2002 Ferrari Enzo was limited to only 399 examples. To quote Ferrari S.p.A., "this car offers drivers the combined experience of multiple consecutive World Constructors' titles with the technical ideas and engine tuning skills of World Champion Michael Schumacher." The Enzo was powered by a naturally aspirated, sixty-five-degree V12 with a completely new design based on Formula One experience. Maximum output was rated at 660 horsepower at 7,800 revolutions per minute. The body styling by Pininfarina was also inspired by Formula One race car design, creating a look never before attempted in a road car.

Following in the footsteps of the 550 Maranello, the 2002 575M Maranello is an even more powerful, more luxurious, sporty, front-engine V12 Berlinetta. With an engine increase to 5,750 cubic centimeters (thus the name), the 575M Maranello offers a significant increase in both power and torque over the 550. The M designation in the model name is for *Modificata*, or modified. Among 575M features is an F1 gearbox with paddle shifters mounted behind the steering wheel. This was first offered on the F355 F1.

The sixty-five-degree V12 in the 575M has four overhead camshafts, four valves per cylinder, and an output of 515 horsepower at 7,250 revolutions per minute.

Maranello's latest offerings include the boldly styled 2007 F430 Berlinetta and Spider.

Also coming for 2007 is the all-new Ferrari Superamerica, resurrecting one of the greatest names in Ferrari history.

The all-new 612 Scaglietti is another uniquely individual model. Named after the great Italian stylist and coachbuilder Sergio Scaglietti, it is the world's first four-seat sport coupe. The 612 features F1 paddle shifters on the steering wheel, and the first application of integrated traction and stability control in a Ferrari. Power comes from a 540-horsepower V12 displacing just under six liters. The 612 Scaglietti is a true grand touring car in the Ferrari tradition.

Just around the corner for 2007 is the magnificent Ferrari 599 GTB Fiorano, the most powerful twelve-cylinder Berlinetta ever developed at Maranello. This new model combines the most innovative and technologically advanced features ever applied by Ferrari to a front-mid engined two-seater, and sets a new benchmark of excellence in terms of handling, driving pleasure, and design. The Fiorano boasts absolutely stunning performance from a six-liter V12, developed from the engine that powered the Enzo supercar, to deliver 620 horsepower at 7,600 revolutions per minute. The Pininfarina-designed Ferrari 599 GTB Fiorano replaces the last in that great line of Berlinettas, the 575M Maranello, of which, together with the 550 Maranello introduced in 1996, no fewer than 5,700 have been produced, a record for this flagship model for the Prancing Horse.

Touring the Ferrari Factory
Home of the Cavallino Rampante

The Ferrari factory is a very modern, very different factory than it was in Enzo Ferrari's day, but the cars that bear his name are still manufactured as handcrafted automobiles.

Far right: It's hands-on as much as possible as cars move slowly down the Ferrari assembly line. While robotics and high-technology manufacturing certainly play a role in building Ferraris today, it is still the hand labor that makes each a work of mechanical art.

Back in 1998, Luigi Chinetti, Jr., and I toured the Ferrari manufacturing facilities in Maranello along with two of our friends, the authors Steve Fjestad and R. L. Wilson. At the time, both Larry Wilson and I were working on new books about the Italian firearms industry, but with Luigi among the group, doors in Maranello opened that would otherwise have been closed to visitors. This afforded me the opportunity to road test the then new 550 Maranello and an early version of the F355 F1, equipped with Formula One–type paddle shifters on the steering column. Luigi and I road-tested the cars through the mountains around Maranello and Modena, and also had use of Ferrari's Fiorano test track. It doesn't get any better than that.

After a day of driving and photography, we were treated the next morning to a tour of the Ferrari assembly lines.

Thinking of Ferrari as an automaker conjures up visions of men carrying out their jobs in small workshops, building chassis, engines, and transmissions by hand, while in nearby Modena, Scaglietti's craftsmen are pounding out aluminum and steel bodies over wooden styling bucks. Factory photographs from the 1950s and '60s will bear evidence to those memories, but that was not the Ferrari we saw toward the end of the twentieth century. Here was a state-of-the-art assembly line, with workmen building Ferraris in series, with one car after another stretching to the far end of the building. Yet it was not mass production, not the way we so often see it portrayed in television commercials with robotic arms welding cars together, sparks flying, and parts moving about in a mechanical ballet. At Maranello,

cars were being assembled by teams of craftsmen, one by one, with almost clocklike precision. It was still very much like the old days, just at a more vigorous pace. Craftsmanship cannot be rushed, even in the twenty-first century.

The Ferrari assembly plant is a self-contained operation with departments tending to individual tasks such as hand-picking leather for seat and interior upholstery and women hand-stitching seat cushions, much the way it was done half a century ago. Engines on individual stands were being hand-fitted together, measured, checked, and rechecked before moving on to the chassis. It truly was what one Ferrari representative explained to me as

During a visit to the factory in 1998, the author watched as this F50 was completed and readied for testing.

A short walk across the street from the factory is the Ferrari Museum in Maranello. In 1997–'98 the museum featured cars from fifty years of Ferrari history.

"the old world and the new world as one." This was the same impression we all had when touring the Italian gunmakers in Brescia, Gardone, later that week. There was modern machinery everywhere to assist in the manufacturing of parts, but the final assembly, the finishing touches required to produce a fine firearm—rifle, pistol, or sporting shotgun—were the same handcrafting techniques that had been used by Italian gunmakers such as Pietro Beretta for centuries. This kind of workmanship was evident in everything we saw in Italy, whether it was a pair of shoes, a suit, a hand-carved cameo, a Beretta shotgun, or a Ferrari 550 Maranello.

A Little Side Trip

Not far from the factory is the Ferrari Museum, a striking structure that is home to Ferrari history. Here one can see the evolution of Ferrari, from the postwar 1940s to the present day, depicted in a stunning array of photographs, documents, and the cars themselves. Walking through the gallery with Luigi, we stopped repeatedly to look at images of his father, Enzo Ferrari, and so many of the great designers, engineers, and drivers who made the Cavallino Rampante legendary, not only in Italy but throughout the world.

Making a trip to Maranello and Modena is both rewarding and enlightening. It is one thing to see a Ferrari on the road, or on the showroom floor of a dealership, it is quite another to see one built, to understand, from a craftsman's perspective, what makes a Ferrari a Ferrari.

Above: The multi-level building always has a variety of significant cars on display, from the worlds of racing and grand touring.

Race driver and race car constructor Luigi Chinetti, Jr., walks along the wall of fame in the Ferrari Museum looking at pictures of his father and then suddenly finds one of himself driving a 365 GTB/4 Daytona to victory at Le Mans in 1971.

Chapter 10

Enzo's Passion—Tales of the Cavallino Rampante

The difference between dreaming and doing is all in the doing.
Enzo Ferrari must have had incredible dreams.

"When I grow up, I'm going to be a racing car driver. When I grow up, I'm going to be a racing car champion." These were the words of a very young Enzo Ferrari, spoken at a time when Italy knew little about the combustion engine or motorized transport and even less about racing cars. It didn't matter. When Enzo Ferrari grew up, he became not only a racing car driver but a force that would forever change race cars, their drivers, and the sport of motor racing. "When I grow up, I'm going to be a racing car driver," said Enzo Ferrari. Truer words were never spoken.

Today the good racing teams consist of owners, designers, mechanics, technicians, and drivers working together. In the pits and garages of the most successful marques, team members share their wisdom. They trade ideas. And they listen to one another. Everyone has a role, and everyone has a voice. In the garages of the Scuderia Ferrari, everyone had a role, but there was only one voice. And it came from the man behind the dark glasses. The only voice that mattered was that of Ferrari.

The 166 MM had a simple, purposeful, yet elegant interior suitable to the needs of either touring the open road, or sliding around a corner in the Targa Florio. (Photograph by Andy Marks)

Left: It was the first great race and road car from Ferrari. The 166 Mille Miglia, or as it became popularly known, the 166 MM Touring Barchetta, established Ferrari as both a constructor of sports and racing cars by 1949.

Luigi Chinetti, Sr., at the wheel of a 166 MM brought Ferrari its most important early postwar victory in the 1949 Le Mans 24 Hours.

Young Enzo's dream of becoming "a racing car driver" was realized in 1919, when he entered, and performed quite handsomely in, a hill climb in Parma. That performance earned him an opportunity to race in the great Italian road race—the Targa Florio—that same year. Twelve months later, Ferrari had driven and talked his way onto the Alfa Romeo team and under the wing of the celebrated driver Giuseppe Campari. While he enjoyed some success as a driver, it was as a team owner that Ferrari would emerge as one of the most accomplished and, at the same time, most feared individuals in the history of organized motor sports.

Enzo Ferrari started racing cars as a team owner when he was forty-nine years old. He stopped when he died at ninety. And for every day of every month of every one of those four decades and a year, Ferrari ruled his racing teams with a fist of iron. Past successes were just that—of the past; if you were so blessed as to wear the Cavallino Rampante on your uniform, you were expected to deliver success on every day. To fail once was to lose the privilege of being part of the Scuderia. To succeed was to earn the chance to stay on until the next race.

Enzo Ferrari was not a man who suffered fools easily. For those unfortunate souls who upset Il Commendatore, the penalty was purgatorial. Even those who served him well were not immune to

One of, if not the most remarkable, body style ever to grace the 166 platform was this racer designed by and bodied for Carlo Abarth. (Photographs by Andy Marks)

his verbal castigation. One may question his methods—and many did. But no one can question his results. The blazing red Ferraris have won more than forty world championships and more than five thousand races. They are the only marque that has actively raced in Formula One since its inception, more than half a century ago. And they are today as large as the legend of the man who was in life, and remains in memory, the passion and the heart of the Scuderia Ferrari. "Racing builds the breed," Ferrari would often say. And the breed of race cars that have worn the black stallion on the yellow shield are among the greatest cars ever to fill a starting grid. And it all started with a little twelve-cylinder powerhouse called "The 125."

It is May 1947 in Piacenza, Italy. Franco Cortese is behind the wheel of the first Ferrari race car—the Tipo 125. Cortese would lead the race for a brief period before mechanical difficulties ended his day. The day may not have concluded in the

Racing was the fundament of Ferrari, both the company and the man. In his early twenties, Enzo Ferrari began his career as a race driver for Alfa Romeo, advancing to team manager, establishing the Scuderia Ferrari, and ultimately his own business as a constructor and automaker.

Below: By the 1950s the Ferrari factory was building a variety of *competizione* models from single-seat Formula race cars to the Testa Rossa.

winner's circle. But it saw the debut of the Scuderia Ferrari. And it was only two weeks later that Cortese would race the 125 to victory at Caracalla in Rome.

The Tipo 125 featured a 1.25-liter, water-cooled V12 designed by Giaocchino Colombo. With an alloy engine block, 6.5:1 compression and five-speed, single-plate clutch transmission, the 710-kilogram racer was capable of 300 horsepower at an engine speed of 7,000 revolutions per minute. But even with 300 brake horsepower at the driver's calling, the 125 was weak and difficult to handle at speed. With the engine reworked and displacement increased to 1.9 liters, the car was rebadged Tipo 159. It now had the strength to compete, but it still lacked stability.

The 125/159 brought only a handful of victories to Ferrari. But what it failed to attract in wins it more than made up for in talent. With Raymond Sommer's victory in the 159 in Turin, Ferrari

For its time, the Testa Rossa was one of the most exciting and powerful race cars ever put into the hands of Ferrari clientele. The examples shown are of the first body configuration by Scaglietti, featuring the full pontoon-style fenders.

was able to retain Colombo while luring Aurelio Lampredi back to Ferrari—the team he had left some years earlier to join Isotta-Fraschini. While Colombo continued to refine the 125/159, Lampredi designed the car that would become the 166. And with the 166 available for customer purchase and street use, Ferrari would watch as his friend and patron Luigi Chinetti, Sr., brought the Scuderia its first major victory at Le Mans with the 166 MM. At this point, the dye was cast, and the name Ferrari was soon to become synonymous with racing greatness.

As the decade of the forties ended, so did the Grand Prix racing

programs at Alfa Romeo and Maserati. With their previous employers no longer on the track, Ferrari was able to enlist the services of two of the best drivers in the world—Alberto Ascari and Gigi Villoresi. Now loaded with a powerful and reliable car and the finest drivers anywhere, Ferrari was ready to take on the world.

Clemente Biondetti won the 1948 Mille Miglia, and Chinetti made his historic Le Mans run in 1949. This Barchetta or "little boat" was pow-

ered by the engine that started out as the 1.25-liter V12 from the Tipo 125. When Formula Two racing regulations that allowed for a larger 2.0-liter engine were enacted for the 1950 season, Ferrari responded by increasing the 1949 engine's bore and stroke from 55 x 52.5 millimeters to 59 x 58 millimeters. By the time the engine found its way into the nose of the 166, stroke had increased to nearly 60, and engine displacement was just five ticks under the 2,000-cubic-centimeter limit.

This was now named the 166 MM, in recognition of Ferrari's victory in the 1948 Mille Miglia; only thirteen examples of the car were built in 1950. Of the twenty-six Tipo 166 models that were built in 1949 and 1950, only six were retained by the Scuderia for racing, with the remaining cars sold to private owners for their personal road use. The ninth 166 MM built in 1950 was completed just in time for Scuderia Ferrari to enter it in that year's 24 Hours

Although the history of Ferrari is laced with tales of its mighty V12s, the 1950s-era Lampredi-designed four-cylinder Ferrari 500 (pictured), 625, and 860 models were then, and remain today, three of the great Ferrari Formula One and Formula Two race cars in the history of the great and storied marque.

of Le Mans. Electronic malfunctions forced the car out early, but a few weeks later that 166 MM would reemerge, with none other than Luigi Chinetti in the driver's seat, to claim the 1,000km race at Montlhéry. A month later, the Ferrari would enjoy a one-two finish as a pair of 166 MMs overpowered the field in the Daily Express Trophy race held at Silverstone.

From the roads back to the Formula circuits, 1952 saw the emergence of the Ferrari 500. Again relying on the design genius of Lampredi, the 500 would prove unbeatable. With one exception, the car would win every Grand Prix race run in 1952 and 1953. With Ascari in the cockpit, Ferrari would win back-to-back Driver's World Championships. By 1955, the engines had grown to 2.5 liters, and Ferrari, with Juan Manuel Fangio in the seat, was once again dominating racing with the Tipo 625. The year 1956 would end with Scuderia Ferrari winning its third World Championship.

The year 1956 would also see another great Ferrari race car and another great Ferrari racing victory. Designed by Pininfarina and built by Scaglietti, the Ferrari 860 was an engineering masterstroke and an unstoppable force at the Sebring 12 Hours race. The 860 was powered by a 3.4-liter, four-cylinder engine that produced 310 horsepower.

Independent front suspension and hydraulic drum brakes at each corner worked in concert to deliver a car that was extremely controlled in all race conditions. When combined with Fangio's unmatched driving ability, the 860 was able to hold off the competition from Aston Martin, Jaguar, and Maserati.

The interior of this 1954 Ferrari 500 was pure race car. Though beautiful from the outside, its design was not suitable to anything but racing.

The Ferrari 500, 625, and 860 were spectacular cars, but they were also historic in that they were powered by an engine that Ferrari was not, at first, altogether excited to build. And, as has been well recorded, that which did not excite Enzo Ferrari rarely, if ever, came to pass. Ferrari had already fallen in love with the big V12 engines. In this case, however, Lampredi, with some help from the FIA was able sway his team owner.

In 1950, Lampredi convinced Ferrari that a smaller, lighter, four-cylinder power plant would be less complicated to build and maintain. Larger cylinders and bigger valves could be designed with a longer stroke, meaning the little four could produce as much torque and horsepower as the massive V12s or even more. That Ferrari believed new FIA regulations regarding engine size and aspiration would soon be coming did not hurt Lampredi's case.

Less than a year after gaining Ferrari's approval to build the engine, the Scuderia had both 2.0-liter and 2.5-liter variants ready for track testing. The Lampredi-designed four-cylinder Ferrari 500, 625, and 860 were then, and remain today, three of the great Ferrari Formula One and Formula Two race cars in the history of the great and storied marque.

Ferrari's racing greatness was not confined to the Formula One and Two series events. While the Cavallino Rampante was dominating that level of competition, winning Driver's and Constructors' ti-

The Lampredi-designed four-cylinder was designed with larger cylinders, bigger valves, and longer stroke, meaning the little four could produce as much torque and horsepower as the massive V12s, or even more. Less than a year after gaining Ferrari's approval to build the engine, the Scuderia had both 2.0-liter and 2.5-liter variants ready for track testing.

tles, another masterpiece from Modena was emerging as one of the greatest race cars the world would ever know. With seating for two and a roof overhead, these were the GTs—the Grand Turismo or Grand Touring cars. And no Ferrari GT is more cherished in the hearts and minds of Ferrari enthusiasts and historians than the 250 GT. There have been bigger, faster, and more powerful Ferrari GT race cars to roar down the straights and scream through the curves, but there has been none more decorated and, at the same time, more perfect in design, than the 250.

There were almost a dozen variants of the 250 produced between 1953 and 1964, each one a finer-tuned evolution of the one before, and nearly all of them were powered by the Colombo-designed V12 engine that debuted in the Tipo 125. While it was not the biggest or

The Tour de France, a name affectionately given the early 250 GT models following their domination of the ten-day race in 1956, remained in production until 1959.

most powerful stallion in the Ferrari stable, this lightweight engine, with output up to 280 brake horsepower, was a perfect complement to the Pinin Farina–designed, Scaglietti-built coachwork.

The 250's résumé is simply a list of the greatest road and endurance races ever run. The Mille Miglia, 12 Hours of Rheims, Tour de France, Carrera PanAmericana, and the coveted Vingt-Quatre Heures du Mans—these are but a few of the races to have been conquered by the Ferrari 250 GTs. This Ferrari was unique also in that it remained in constant production for over a decade—something that was unheard of at the time. Throughout its run, the 250 GT was constantly being tuned and refined.

The 250 GT Short Wheelbase Berlinetta was the consummate race and road car in the late 1950s and early 1960s. In 1961, Stirling Moss, driving Rob Walker's SWB, won the Tourist Trophy for Ferrari a second time. During the 1961 season so many class wins were collected by SWB Berlinettas, Ferrari claimed the GT class in the Constructors' Championship.

Headlights were recessed and subsequently placed behind Plexiglas in order to cheat the wind. The panels around and over the rear wheels were shortened, extended, and then shortened again as the Scuderia experimented with different shapes and forms. Throughout the production life of the 250 GT, however, the Pinin Farina design and Scaglietti body were the pride of Maranello and the terror of competitors in any race in which the car appeared.

In his first full decade as a constructor and team owner, Ferrari surpassed even his own lofty dreams. On every racing circuit and road course, the Scuderia Ferrari was the star. The cars and engines that came out of Maranello during the middle decade of the

Some consider the 250 GTO to be the greatest sports racing car of all time. The *Gran Turismo Omologato* became the preeminent Ferrari road and race car. Only thirty-nine were produced through 1964, by which time the cars brought Ferrari the coveted Manufacturer's World Championship of sports cars three times—1962, 1963, and 1964—and a total of twenty first-place finishes in twenty-eight races, fifteen seconds, and nine thirds! (Photographs by Dennis Adler and Andy Marks)

twentieth century were legends in their own time. The most skilled drivers, the most gifted designers and engineers—they all worked for Ferrari.

The fifties witnessed staggering success for Ferrari, the man and the team, but they also brought great misfortune. Ferrari's beloved son Dino passed away in 1956. A year later, the Ferrari driver Eugenio Castelotti was killed during testing, and, in that same year, the Marquis de Portago crashed his Ferrari at the Mille Miglia, causing the deaths of twelve spectators and a charge of manslaughter to be brought against Enzo Ferrari. It was these events, many believe, that would, more than any others, haunt Ferrari for the rest of his life.

As the decade turned, the Federation Internationale de L'Automobile started to change the rules of racing in an effort to level the playing field. By 1960, races were being run in order to determine who would finish first—*behind* Ferrari. New regulations set to take effect in 1962 forced Ferrari to charge his chief engineer and designer—Bizzarini and Scaglietti—to come up with a Grand Tourer that would enable Ferrari to maintain its dominance under the stricter regulations.

Ferrari demanded that the new car be small and light and based on the 250 GT Short Wheelbase Berlinetta that had brought such great fortune to Maranello. Ferrari got what he asked for, and the world got what many consider to be the greatest Ferrari ever built— the 250 GTO. The GTO remains today one of the most valuable collector cars in the world. Only thirty-nine were built and all are accounted for.

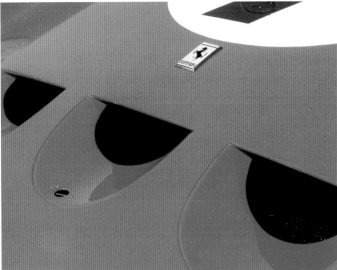

While Ferrari never demanded that the car be beautiful, a magnificent and heretofore unimaginable aerodynamic form emerged out of its spectacular function. Enzo Ferrari had always been "an engine guy." He figured that, if all else failed, he'd have the power to take on and defeat any competitor. But wind tunnel testing and aerodynamics were now taking on a bigger role in race car design. Ferrari begrudgingly recognized that to maintain his dominance on the tracks and road courses, he'd have to begin to consider the car's physical form at least as much as he did its mechanical function. The GTO may have been an evolutionary step forward in engineering from the GT, but it was a revolutionary leap in aerodynamic design.

Back on the Formula One tracks, the Ferraris were being driven by Phil Hill and Wolfgang Von Trips. The 246 debuted in 1960 with high hopes but could not mount a serious assault on the championship. Rear-engine cars were the new standard of excellence, and the front-engine 246 was simply too old to compete for the top spot.

Two very different generations of cars but both representing the epitome of Ferrari design in their time. The 1962 250 GTO (right) and the 2002 Ferrari Enzo. (Photograph by Andy Marks)

A new team engineer—Carlo Chiti—and the need for a car that could compete within the new 1.5-liter Formula One regulations resulted in the Ferrari 156 "Sharknose." The tubular frame of the car was not revolutionary, but it was adequate and serviceable. The crown jewel of the Sharknose was its power plant. A six-cylinder unit with two banks of three cylinders each positioned in a 120-degree V was developed to conform to the new FIA regulations. With the cylinders pushed out to 120 degrees, the entire engine featured a much lower center of gravity. Strategic use of alloys also rendered the engine 30 pounds lighter than those being used by most of the competition.

A new engine in a new car with Hill and Von Trips at the controls proved to be a virtually unbeatable combination. Out of the seven races the 156 entered, five ended with victory. At Spa, the Caval-

lino Rampante finished first through fourth and dominated the race from start to finish. By season's end, the question was not whether Ferrari would win yet another World Championship. The question was whether the title would go to Von Trips or Hill, as both were enjoying great success with the Sharknose Ferrari. Hill had three victories to Von Trips' two when they arrived at Monza to settle the issue. Phil Hill ended up taking the title when his teammate crashed, tragically killing fourteen spectators and losing his own life as well. Once again, history would bestow great success and tragic misfortune concurrently upon the house at Maranello.

Soon after the championship and heartbreak of 1961, Scuderia Ferrari would experience a major internal upheaval. Discord was rampant, and Enzo Ferrari was left to fume as Giotto Bizzarini; Carlo Chiti; the team manager, Romolo Tavoni; and a host of other key racing personnel said good-bye to the Cavallino Rampante. This internal strife would render 1962 and 1963 little more than rebuilding years for Ferrari in Formula One.

The years were not a total loss, however, as the famed 250 GTO was being entered in race after race. Because it was the dominant car of the day, it was not uncommon for half the field to consist of this ultimate Ferrari Grand Turismo! And for those blessed to have a GTO at their disposal, the only competition was whoever showed up with another one. There was simply nothing else that could compete with the Bizzarini-Scaglietti masterpiece.

The 1962, 1963, and 1964 seasons saw Ferrari claim three consecutive Manufacturer's Championship trophies. Although most of the race victories were won by private teams, as the Scuderia was focused primarily on Formula One, Ferrari did provide support and remain actively involved in this branch of the racing tree.

To say the cars were dominant is a study in understatement. North America, Africa, Europe—it didn't matter where they were. Hill climbs, endurance races (including victories at Le Mans, Daytona, and Sebring)—it didn't matter what the event. Even the off-road rallies and the sprints were being commanded by the monstrous GTOs. By 1963, however, the competition was catching up, with lightweight Jaguar E-Types, Chevrolet Corvettes, and Carroll Shelby's AC Cobras now challenging the Ferraris. The cars ended up competing in 107 races that year, claiming an astounding 73 class wins and 22 overall victories. As if

it needed any more affirmation, the GTO was established as the greatest of the great Ferraris when the cars duplicated their first through third finish from a year earlier at Le Mans, to close out the 1963 season.

By 1964, Ferrari had regained its footing in Formula One with a new V8 engine designed by Angelo Bellei. While Jim Clark's Lotus was a faster vehicle, it was also more temperamental: a trait that would enable John Surtees to claim yet another Driver's World Championship for Enzo Ferrari and his Scuderia. It would be the last Formula One World Championship enjoyed by Ferrari for eleven years—the longest drought to date in the team's history.

By 1965, yet more changes in FIA rules precluded the development of a new car. At the same time, Enzo Ferrari was distracted by an inquisitive Ford Motor Company, which was considering acquiring the great Italian marque. The company was becoming increasingly focused

Left-hand or right-hand drive, and in various interior configurations often designed to suit the individual tastes of the driver, the 250 GTO was a blank sheet of paper upon which engineers and race drivers penned the greatest design of the early 1960s. (Photographs by Dennis Adler and Andy Marks)

Victorious noses. A brace of 250 GTOs on exhibit at the 2005 Concourso Italiano in Carmel, California. (Photograph by Andy Marks)

was hired on to share driving duties with Lorenzo Bandini, but the partnership would last only a few weeks; Bandini died three days after crashing and incinerating his car at Monaco. The former Ferrari engineer Mike Parks was brought back to replace Bandini, but his short-lived Formula One racing career ended when a crash at Spa cost him the use of his legs. Once again in need of a driver, Enzo Ferrari enlisted Jacky Ickx before the 1968 season, but the cars were not up to the task, and 1968 and '69 would come and go without Ferrari even coming close to another World Championship.

By 1970, Ferrari had sold the customer car side of his empire to Fiat for nearly $11 million. With new capital in pocket and a new resolve once again to dominate Formula One racing, Il Commendatore stepped in and began to rebuild his beloved racing program. For the next three years, Ferrari worked to develop and refine their new flat-twelve engine. No championships were won, but, once again, Ferraris were proving to be the fastest cars of the day.

For the 1973 season, Enzo Ferrari seized complete and total control of the situation. Colombo was dismissed, Luca Cordero Di Montezemolo (later to become president and CEO of Ferrari S.p.A.) was put in charge of the team, and the driver Niki Lauda was hired. Running the Ferrari 312B3, Lauda claimed victories in Spain and Holland to go with his co-driver Clay Regazzoni's win in Germany. Ferrari was once again poised to take control of the Formula One racing league.

on other racing venues, largely because of the successes being enjoyed by the GTOs, and, as a result, the remainder of the sixties would pass without Ferrari coming anywhere close to the Formula One success they had enjoyed in the previous years.

Constant turnover at the senior levels within Scuderia Ferrari created a caustic atmosphere among those sporting the Cavallino Rampante on their white team uniforms. John Surtees left the team. Eugenio Dragoni was fired and replaced by Franco Lini. Chris Amon

And in 1974, control was theirs. The flat twelve had been redesigned with a transverse gearbox and was loaded back into the now named 312T. Lauda did the rest, winning five races and Ferrari's first Driver's World Championship in more than a decade. Winning two-thirds of the races entered at the beginning of the season, Ferrari and Lauda arrived at the midpoint of the campaign with twice the points of their nearest competitor. But, once again, crises would intersect with success when Lauda crashed at the Nürburgring and had to be pulled from the flaming wreckage that used to be his Ferrari 312.

In what is now part of Formula One lore, Lauda was back and racing a mere six weeks later, and by the time he arrived in Japan for the final race of the year, he was in contention for yet another Driver's title. It was not to be, however, as Lauda had to withdraw from the race, suffering from mechanical and braking disorders. Ferrari did take the Constructors' title that year, so all was not a total loss.

The 1977 season would see a scarred but no less skilled Lauda return to the winner's circle three times and end with him claiming his second World Championship in three years. But by now Lauda had grown tired of the turmoil and tragedy that seemed to plague the Scuderia. He departed Maranello to join on with the Brabham team and left Enzo Ferrari once again looking for a new driver. Unable to attract the proven champions he targeted, Ferrari settled on an upstart Canadian named Gilles Villeneuve. It was a second choice that would pay handsome dividends.

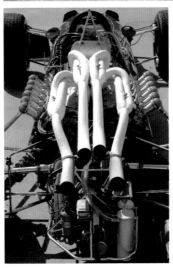

Ferrari's domain encompassed everything from sports car racing to Formula One, and of the latter, the Tipo 312 F1, c.1967–68, was one of the most visually striking, with its tangle of exhausts and twelve carburetors jutting from the sides of the 48-valve V12 engine. Among notable drivers were the legendary Jacky Ickx and Chris Amon. (Photographs by Andy Marks)

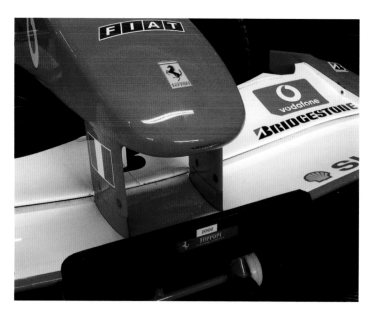

While the 1978 season was not a huge success, it did show Villeneuve to be one of the most fearless drivers to run for the Cavallino Rampante since the great Tazio Nuvolari had handled the wheel some fifty years earlier. Villeneuve's first victory did not come until the end of the season, when he triumphed in Canada. While Enzo Ferrari could not claim the World Championship as his own, he knew he had the driver who would soon deliver the goods.

And deliver he did, with four race victories in 1979. Villeneuve's teammate Jody Scheckter ended up winning the title, however, having accumulated more points. But throughout the season, the Ferrari 312T4 designed by Mauro Forghieri was proving to be a sound car on which to rebuild the Ferrari racing dynasty.

Forghieri had been promoted to the head position in charge of Ferrari racing years earlier, at the tender age of twenty-six. Now experienced and well into his forties, Forghieri had a keen understanding of engine dynamics and aerodynamic design. The sleek body and flat twelve were now dominating the tracks and returning championships to Italy and Ferrari. But success would once again be short-lived. The Scuderia would enter the eighties unable to catch the British team, who had scored significant advances in the wind tunnel, which translated into numerous victories on the race circuits. Villeneuve was able to savor victory in the two races at Monaco and Spain that year, but there would be no repeat of the championship won during the previous year's Formula One campaign.

By 1982, Ferrari had replaced the 312 with the 126C. The chassis dynamics and body aerodynamics now matched the engine in excellence, and Ferrari was once again the team to watch. But success was not to be. Enzo's young protégé Villeneuve—the man who reminded so many of the great Nuvolari—would die in a crash two weeks after the San Marino Grand Prix as he prepared for the race at Imola. The year that was to bring another Driver's Championship to the Cavallino Rampante turned into another year of loss.

Ferrari would win two more Constructors' Championships in 1983 and '84. They would also hire driver Mario Andretti to replace Didier Pironi, whose Formula One career ended when he destroyed his legs in a crash at Hockenheim. And the team would continue, under the increasingly angered eyes of Enzo Ferrari, to try to find the winning formula of engine, body, and driver.

By the mid-eighties, the racing world seemed to have caught up to Ferrari. Teams from McLaren-TAG and Williams-Honda matched Ferrari for engine power while surpassing them in the study and application of aerodynamic design and downforce. As it had so many times before, political infighting was crippling the Ferrari organization. New engineers were hired away from the competition, but Enzo could not assemble that right mix of engine power, chassis design, and human talent to bring the World Championship home once more to Maranello.

With tensions dying down and the Ferraris beginning to win races again, it appeared that success was at hand as Scuderia Ferrari took the checkered flag in the last two races of the 1987 season.

Unfortunately, the personality conflicts continued through the 1988 season. Drivers and engineers argued over engines and chassis. Ferrari, now ninety years old, would fire his own son Piero Lardi Ferrari and turn management of the racing team over to the Fiat executive Giorgio Cappelli, while the renowned British engineer Dr. Harvey Postlethwaite, who had joined Ferrari in 1981, left the team to join Tyrell. Enzo Ferrari thought that, maybe now, he had the right mix of mechanical, aerodynamic, and human resources to put together a World Championship run. He would never find out.

On Sunday, August 14, 1988, Enzo Ferrari died. The force behind the most storied and decorated racing organization the world had ever known was gone. The insatiable will to win was not unique to Enzo Ferrari, but his very presence was a key to turn winning desires into championship reality. While strong leadership and top-flight technology were still in place within Scuderia Ferrari, the loss of Il Commendatore was for the moment irreconcilable. Racing was the very heart and soul of Enzo Ferrari, and he, in turn, the heart, soul, and passion of the Scuderia. It was his obsessive desire for racing superiority that pushed the entire team to never before seen levels of greatness.

Ferrari has owned Formula One for more years than any other manufacturer. Seen here is champion Ferrari driver Michael Schumacher and his F1.

Schumacher at speed.

The early nineties saw Ferrari continue to make improvements in their cars while they shuffled the management and engineering personnel who oversaw team operations. These small successes caught the eye of a young German driver who would join Scuderia Ferrari in time for the 1996 season. The driver brought high hopes and great expectations to Maranello. His name was Michael Schumacher.

In spite of gearbox problems that plagued the team throughout the year, Schumacher scored impressive victories at the Grand Prix in Belgium, Spain, and at Monza. By 1997, the Ferrari F310 had evolved into a tremendously competitive ride, and the German phenom was able to capture four more checkered flags and nearly win the Driver's World Championship. The 1998 and 1999 seasons would see Scuderia Ferrari become a force to be reckoned with as they entered the final race of the year fighting for the 1999 world title. The 1999 Constructors' title win set the stage for Ferrari's return to greatness just as a new century was about to dawn.

Michael Schumacher was going to bring the World Championship back to Maranello. Everyone inside and outside the Ferrari team knew it. He had the nerve and driving skills, and, equally as important, Ferrari finally had the cars it needed to put their driver at the front of the pack. And in 2000, it happened. Twenty-one years removed from Scheckter's title of 1979, Schumacher collected his third Driver's Championship. It was the tenth championship for the Scuderia Ferrari but the team's first in more than two decades.

For the next three years, the Ferraris, piloted by Schumacher and Rubens Barrichello, would rewrite the record books. The 2001 season brought "The Shoe" his fourth Driver's World Championship, to go with Ferrari's second consecutive Constructor's title. The season ended with Schumacher claiming his fifth title while Ferrari dominated the Formula One series as no team ever had prior, winning fifteen of the seventeen races in which they competed. Schumacher took the winner's trophy an astounding eleven times, while his partner, Barrichello, claimed four victories for himself and for the house of Maranello.

In 2003, Schumacher surpassed the great (and former Ferrari team driver) Juan Manuel Fangio when he claimed his record sixth Driver's World Championship while bestowing the Constructors' title upon the Cavallino Rampante for the fifth consecutive year. Ferrari was back. While Il Commendatore was not there to bear witness, it was as if he were commanding his racing forces from above.

In a manner not seen since the late fifties, races were being run to determine who would take second place. A Ferrari on the starting grid all but guaranteed that a Ferrari would be parking in the winner's circle at day's end. And just in case there was anyone left on the planet who did not believe that Ferrari was the greatest marque in the history of racing, the 2004 season would end with Schumacher winning thirteen of eighteen races and Ferrari racking up more than twice as many podium finish points as their next closest competitor and claiming yet another World Championship.

The most significant names in motor sports are names listed in the Scuderia Ferrari lifetime team roster. From the driver's seat and from the pits, the greatest innovators and most fearless pilots pushed Ferrari, and all of racing for that matter, to higher levels. The Scuderia Ferrari was sometimes an innovator and at other times an imitator. But it was always a force to be feared. Automobile racing, and Formula One racing specifically, may be bigger than any single team or any one man. But it's impossible to imagine what auto racing would be like had a young resident of Maranello not declared, "When I grow up, I'm going to be a racing car driver."

The star of Ferrari's late-twentieth- and early-twenty-first-century racing efforts, Michael Schumacher.

Nothing can quite equal the spirited reverberation of a twelve-cylinder Ferrari engine at full throttle, bellowing tenor exhaust notes that resonate in the air and rumble through your body with the unrelenting thump of a distant drum. Surround this sensation with exquisite, hand-built coachwork, and you have one of automotive history's great combinations of lust and poetry.

Ferraris are a passion, and passion knows no bounds. For nearly sixty years the cars with the yellow-and-black Cavallino Rampante emblem have represented the ultimate expression of speed and automotive sensuality. Throughout the last six decades, they have been compared to the muscular stature of an athlete, the grace and speed of a thoroughbred, and the beauty of a woman's body. And, moreover, Ferraris have been the yardstick by which all other sports cars have been measured for more than half a century.

My dear late friend and writing partner T. C. Browne noted some years ago that scholars throughout the world agreed Ferrari is the most recognized Italian word. We celebrate the Ferrari legend in *The Road From Maranello*, a road paved by triumph, tragedy, and genius. We honor both a man and his machines, and all that they have meant to sports car enthusiasts since Enzo Ferrari lent his name to the first Tipo 125 Sport, in 1947.

Enzo Ferrari had many gifts, talents that he used to his advantage. Though he was a skilled driver with numerous victories to his credit, Ferrari's greatest talent was his ability to take command and direct others, whether it was leading the Alfa Romeo race team or building a race car. Wrote Enzo of his own attributes and innate talent for "stirring up" men, "I have never considered myself as a designer or inventor, but only one who gets things moving and keeps them

The author at South Bay Studio in Long Beach, California, photographing the Henry Ford II Barchetta for *Ferrari: The Road from Maranello.*

running." That "innate talent" enabled Enzo Ferrari to surround himself with talented people throughout his career. The names of engineers such as Gioacchino Colombo, Vittorio Jano, and Aurelio Lampredi, and the designers Carlo Felice Bianchi Anderloni, Battista Pinin Farina, Sergio Scaglietti, Mario and Gian Paolo Boano, and Sergio Pininfarina have become as much a part of Ferrari lore as the cars themselves. And let us not forget the greatest Ferraristi of all, the late Luigi Chinetti, Sr., without whose efforts there would likely be little, if anything, to write about today.

Ferraris are among the most written about, but also most difficult to understand, sports cars in automotive history, and it is with great respect that I mention those authors who have driven along this path of confusion that leads from Maranello. Most notable is the work of Antoine Prunet, who has made understanding Ferrari history a crusade; the late Hans Tanner, who with Doug Nye created the most comprehensive early history of the marque ever written and a must-have reference on Ferrari racing; and, of course, my very first editor, the late Dean Batchelor, whose excellent Ferrari books have become standard references the world over.

Additional research for this book came from a remarkable two-volume set, *Ferrari Catalogue Raisonné,* published in Italy by Automobilia; and *Ferrari—Design of a Legend: The Official History and Catalog*, by Gianni Rogliatti, Sergio Pininfarina, and Valerio Moretti, published by Abbeville Press; and *The Enzo Ferrari Memoirs—My Terrible Joys* by Enzo Ferrari (London: Motoraces Book Club, Hamish Hamilton, 1965).

Others who have contributed to the content of this book include the inimitable Denise McCluggage, one of the first women to race for Ferrari under the NART banner, and the legendary photographer and author Henry Rasmussen. A special note of thanks is also due to my agent, Peter Riva, who has stood behind me (and often pushed me) for the last eight years and through the trials of writing my last six books. You know the old saying, "Behind every successful man there is a great woman"; well, behind every successful author there is a great agent. I would also like to thank my very talented and tireless art director, Keith Betterley; my terrific research associate Andy Marks; the Robert M. Lee Collection and Scott Bergan; Dick Messer and the Petersen Automotive Museum; Skeets Dunn; David Sydorick; Sam and Emily Mann; my friend and occasional Italian interpreter: Luigi "Coco" Chinetti, Jr.; the incomparable R. L. Wilson; the late Greg Garrison, who was a wonderful friend and great Ferrari enthusiast; Dr. Ron Busuttil; Chip Connor; and my buddy and consummate car guy, Bruce Meyer, without whose generous help this book would be lacking a certain number of spectacular cars.

Index

Page numbers in *italics* refer to illustrations.

Dennis Adler is recognized as one of the leading automotive journalists in the world. He is editor at large for *Car Collector* magazine, senior editor of the Mercedes-Benz publication *The Star,* and the author of more than twenty-five books. His previous books include *The Art of the Automobile: The 100 Greatest Cars, The Art of the Sports Car,* and *Porsche: The Road from Zuffenhausen.* A native Californian, he now lives in Pennsylvania.